Family Violence

Other Books of Related Interest:

At Issue Series

Child Labor and Sweatshops

Do Children Have Rights?

Should Juveniles Be Given Life Without Parole?

Current Controversies Series

The Elderly

Teen Pregnancy and Parenting

Introducing Issues with Opposing Viewpoints Series

Child Abuse

Opposing Viewpoints Series

Child Custody

The Taliban

Family Violence

Diane Andrews Henningfeld, Book Editor

GREENHAVEN PRESS
A part of Gale, Cengage Learning

Detroit • New York • San Francisco • New Haven, Conn • Waterville, Maine • London

Elizabeth Des Chenes, *Managing Editor*

© 2012 Greenhaven Press, a part of Gale, Cengage Learning

Gale and Greenhaven Press are registered trademarks used herein under license.

For more information, contact:
Greenhaven Press
27500 Drake Rd.
Farmington Hills, MI 48331-3535
Or you can visit our Internet site at gale.cengage.com

ALL RIGHTS RESERVED.
No part of this work covered by the copyright herein may be reproduced, transmitted, stored, or used in any form or by any means graphic, electronic, or mechanical, including but not limited to photocopying, recording, scanning, digitizing, taping, Web distribution, information networks, or information storage and retrieval systems, except as permitted under Section 107 or 108 of the 1976 United States Copyright Act, without the prior written permission of the publisher.

For product information and technology assistance, contact us at

Gale Customer Support, 1-800-877-4253
For permission to use material from this text or product, submit all requests online at www.cengage.com/permissions

Further permissions questions can be emailed to permissionrequest@cengage.com

Articles in Greenhaven Press anthologies are often edited for length to meet page requirements. In addition, original titles of these works are changed to clearly present the main thesis and to explicitly indicate the author's opinion. Every effort is made to ensure that Greenhaven Press accurately reflects the original intent of the authors. Every effort has been made to trace the owners of copyrighted material.

Cover image copyright © ZouZou/Shutterstock.com.

LIBRARY OF CONGRESS CATALOGING-IN-PUBLICATION DATA

Family violence / Diane Andrews Henningfeld, book editor.
 p. cm. -- (Global viewpoints)
 Includes bibliographical references and index.
 ISBN 978-0-7377-5650-0 (hardcover) -- ISBN 978-0-7377-5651-7 (pbk.)
 1. Family violence--Case studies. 2. Family violence--Prevention. I. Henningfeld, Diane Andrews.
 HV6626.F336 2012
 362.82'92--dc23
                                                              2011026844

Printed in the USA
2 3 4 5 6   30 29 28 27 26

Contents

Foreword	11
Introduction	14

Chapter 1: Family Violence and Intimate Partner Abuse

1. Family Violence in the **United States**: An Overview   21
   The National Center for Victims of Crime
   Domestic violence can be defined as abusive behavior by a family member, a household member, or an intimate partner toward another in an attempt to exert power or control. All members of the family or household are affected by violence within the group.

2. In **Ireland**, Women Bear the Brunt of Family Violence   31
   Carol Hunt
   Although some men claim otherwise, data collected in Ireland and throughout the world evidences that women overwhelmingly outnumber men as victims of spousal abuse; suggesting otherwise is "tragic and irresponsible."

3. In **Australia**, Some Men Are Abused by Their Intimate Partners   38
   Andrea Mayes
   A 2010 study provides evidence that Australian men suffer violence from their intimate partners but rarely report it. Such abuse often takes the form of emotional abuse, rather than physical, and has long-lasting effects on the victim.

4. In **Nigeria**, Family Violence Affects Many Women   46
   IRIN
   Up to two-thirds of women in Nigeria's largest city are victims of some type of abuse from family members. Amnesty International is urging the Nigerian government to enact laws to end such violence.

5. In **Vietnam**, Many Women Are Abused by Their Partners 51
   General Statistics Office of Vietnam
   More than half of all Vietnamese women report physical, sexual, or emotional violence at the hands of their partners, according to a new study.

6. In **Scotland**, Many Victims of Family Violence Remain Silent 56
   Tanya Thompson
   Middle-class Scottish women are reluctant to reveal spousal abuse for fear of being stigmatized by their peers. A new program has been launched to raise awareness and offer help.

7. In **Japan**, Spousal Abuse Remains Hidden 64
   David McNeill and Chie Matsumoto
   Despite a 2001 domestic violence law that criminalized spousal abuse in Japan, many women are afraid to reveal that they are the victims of abuse.

8. In the **United States**, Lesbian, Gay, Bisexual, and Transgender (LGBT) People Experience Intimate Partner Abuse 71
   National Coalition of Anti-Violence Programs et al.
   The results of a 2007 study reveal that members of the LGBT community both perpetrate and suffer violence at the hands of intimate partners in significant numbers.

Periodical and Internet Sources Bibliography 78

Chapter 2: Dowry Violence, Bride Burning, and Honor Killings

1. In **Pakistan**, Dowry Disputes Lead to Violence 80
   Rakhshinda Parveen
   Jahez, or dowry, is a cultural custom in Pakistan that often leads to violence and death for the bride, although such deaths are generally underreported.

2. In **India**, Bride Burning Is a Significant Problem 89
Nehaluddin Ahmad

A significant and growing number of young Indian women are burned alive, beaten to death, or pushed to commit suicide by their husbands' families in disputes about money the bride brings to the family in a custom known as "dowry."

3. In **Bangladesh**, the Custom of Dowry Leads to Abuse 95
Kaushalya Ruwanthika Ariyathilaka

Although Bangladesh has prohibited the practice of dowry since 1980, the custom is still widely practiced, often leading to serious abuse of wives from poor families.

4. In **Iraq**, Honor Killings Subjugate Women 105
Terri Judd

Young women in Iraq and Kurdistan are subject to murder by their families for speaking with, telephoning, or falling in love with men not selected by their families. Honor killing is not outlawed in Iraq.

5. The **United States** Should Differentiate Honor Killings from Domestic Violence 110
Phyllis Chesler

Honor killings are essentially different from spousal and child abuse in that they are religiously based, and the motivation for the murders is family honor. The United States must provide support and shelter specifically for women in danger of honor slaying.

6. **Jordan** Cracks Down on Honor Killings 122
Tom Peter

As a result of the way Jordan handles honor killings, much longer sentences are given to men who commit such murders; many hope Jordan's example will influence others in the region.

Periodical and Internet Sources Bibliography 128

Chapter 3: Family Violence and Children

1. In **China** and Other **Asian** Countries, Girl Babies Are the Victims of Family Violence — 130
   The Economist
   In countries such as China, India, Taiwan, Singapore, and South Korea, many more boys than girls are being born and surviving to adulthood because girl babies are selectively aborted, killed within days of birth, or ill-treated by parents throughout childhood.

2. The World Health Organization Calls for the Elimination of Female Genital Mutilation — 138
   The World Health Organization
   Female genital mutilation is the practice of partial or total removal of female genital organs in girls, ordered by and/or carried out by members of their families. The practice is common in many places throughout the world.

3. In **Uganda**, the Practice of Female Genital Mutilation Continues Despite the Law — 147
   Frederick Womakuyu
   The Ugandan Parliament passed a law in 2010 banning the practice of female genital mutilation (FGM); however, elders in some districts claim that FGM is a cultural tradition that they will continue.

4. Female Genital Mutilation Is Practiced in Parts of **Europe** — 153
   Laura Schweiger
   Although female genital mutilation is more widely associated with Africa and the Middle East, the European Union estimates that some five hundred thousand girls in Europe have been subjected to or are in danger of this practice at the insistence of their families.

5. Divorce Can Lead to Violence Directed at Children — 159
   Graeme Hamilton
   A judge's ruling concerning custody in a contentious Canadian divorce leads to the death of one child and the serious wounding of another.

6. Parricide in the **United States** 164
Kathleen M. Heide
About five parents per week are killed by their children in the United States. These children have been severely abused, are dangerously antisocial, or are seriously mentally ill.

Periodical and Internet Sources Bibliography 177

Chapter 4: Family Violence and Elders

1. Elders Must Seek Help When Abused 179
Weill Cornell Medical College
Elder abuse usually means that one family member is inflicting physical, emotional, or financial pain on another family member who is elderly. Older adults who suspect they are being abused must speak up and seek help.

2. In **India**, the Abuse of Older People by Family Members Is Increasing 187
Mala Kapur Shankardass
Abuse and neglect of the elderly is considered a "normal consequence" of aging. Women in particular must plan for their old age while they are still young to avoid family violence.

3. In **Israel**, Family Members Abuse and Neglect the Elderly 193
Judy Siegel-Itzkovich
As Israeli society ceases to honor the elders in their population, the incidence of family violence directed toward the elderly is becoming more widespread.

4. In **Malaysia**, Elder Abuse Must Be Reported and Prevented 201
Esther G. Ebenezer
The growth of the elderly population in Malaysia means that the potential for more abuse of older adults exists. Learning the signs of abuse and intervening on behalf of the older person is vital.

5. Some Chinese Senior Citizens in the **United States** Suffer Elder Abuse	**208**
Rong Xiaoqing	
Because Chinese culture values family unity, identifying and intervening in cases of elder abuse is difficult in this community.	
Periodical and Internet Sources Bibliography	**215**
For Further Discussion	**216**
Organizations to Contact	**218**
Bibliography of Books	**223**
Index	**226**

Foreword

> "The problems of all of humanity can only be solved by all of humanity."
> —Swiss author Friedrich Dürrenmatt

Global interdependence has become an undeniable reality. Mass media and technology have increased worldwide access to information and created a society of global citizens. Understanding and navigating this global community is a challenge, requiring a high degree of information literacy and a new level of learning sophistication.

Building on the success of its flagship series, Opposing Viewpoints, Greenhaven Press has created the Global Viewpoints series to examine a broad range of current, often controversial topics of worldwide importance from a variety of international perspectives. Providing students and other readers with the information they need to explore global connections and think critically about worldwide implications, each Global Viewpoints volume offers a panoramic view of a topic of widespread significance.

Drugs, famine, immigration—a broad, international treatment is essential to do justice to social, environmental, health, and political issues such as these. Junior high, high school, and early college students, as well as general readers, can all use Global Viewpoints anthologies to discern the complexities relating to each issue. Readers will be able to examine unique national perspectives while, at the same time, appreciating the interconnectedness that global priorities bring to all nations and cultures.

Material in each volume is selected from a diverse range of sources, including journals, magazines, newspapers, nonfiction books, speeches, government documents, pamphlets, organization newsletters, and position papers. Global Viewpoints is truly global, with material drawn primarily from international sources available in English and secondarily from US sources with extensive international coverage.

Features of each volume in the Global Viewpoints series include:

- An **annotated table of contents** that provides a brief summary of each essay in the volume, including the name of the country or area covered in the essay.

- An **introduction** specific to the volume topic.

- A **world map** to help readers locate the countries or areas covered in the essays.

- For each viewpoint, an **introduction** that contains notes about the author and source of the viewpoint explains why material from the specific country is being presented, summarizes the main points of the viewpoint, and offers three **guided reading questions** to aid in understanding and comprehension.

- **For further discussion** questions that promote critical thinking by asking the reader to compare and contrast aspects of the viewpoints or draw conclusions about perspectives and arguments.

- A worldwide list of **organizations to contact** for readers seeking additional information.

- A **periodical bibliography** for each chapter and a **bibliography of books** on the volume topic to aid in further research.

- A comprehensive **subject index** to offer access to people, places, events, and subjects cited in the text, with the countries covered in the viewpoints highlighted.

Foreword

Global Viewpoints is designed for a broad spectrum of readers who want to learn more about current events, history, political science, government, international relations, economics, environmental science, world cultures, and sociology—students doing research for class assignments or debates, teachers and faculty seeking to supplement course materials, and others wanting to understand current issues better. By presenting how people in various countries perceive the root causes, current consequences, and proposed solutions to worldwide challenges, Global Viewpoints volumes offer readers opportunities to enhance their global awareness and their knowledge of cultures worldwide.

Introduction

> "Family violence can be found in every country in the world, cutting across gender and all racial, ethnic, religious and socioeconomic lines. Although case definitions vary from culture to culture, family violence represents a major public health problem by virtue of the many deaths, injuries, and adverse psychological consequences that it causes."
>
> —World Medical Association, "WMA Statement on Family Violence," October 2010. www.wma.net.

Family violence is a broad term that encompasses a number of violent acts committed between members of a family. Such violence can cause serious emotional and physical damage to the victim; in some cases, this damage can be so extreme that it results in death. Throughout the world, family violence is increasing. It can include spousal or intimate partner assault, rape, or mental abuse. In Ireland, for example, one in seven women suffers serious violence at the hands of her intimate partner, according to the Economic and Social Research Institute/National Crime Council's 2005 report, "Domestic Abuse of Women and Men in Ireland: Report on the National Study of Domestic Abuse."

The term also applies to the physical, sexual, or mental abuse or neglect of children in a family setting. Throughout the world, many children are affected. As reported in the *Hürriyet Daily News* of April 23, 2011, for example, research in Turkey revealed that "thirty-two percent of children are exposed to violence by either their mother or father at least once a week."

Another form family violence can take is the abuse or neglect of elderly parents or relatives at the hands of partners, spouses, or younger family members. (The National Institute of Justice, part of the US Department of Justice, notes that 57 percent of the perpetrators of elder abuse were partners or spouses.) The problem is expected to grow for two reasons. First, according to the 2007 article "Elder Abuse" by the National Institute of Justice, "In the United States, the issue of elder mistreatment is garnering the attention of the law enforcement, medical, and research communities as more people are living longer than ever before." Second, there will be far more elderly people as the postwar baby boom generation reaches old age.

Although family violence is widespread in nearly every culture in the world, in most circumstances, it has been considered a private matter for the family to deal with without the intervention of outside parties. For this reason, family violence of all sorts is largely underreported. As Vice Admiral Richard H. Carmona, MD, the surgeon general of the United States, stated in his 2003 speech "Family Violence as a Public Health Issue," "Victims are often afraid or unwilling to report it, and as a society we are still too reluctant to discuss it. The silence and secrecy that still surround the issue make it very difficult to face." Nonetheless, family violence has huge implications and consequences for society at large, and thus must be addressed through national and international public health channels such as the Centers for Disease Control and Prevention (CDC) in the United States or the World Health Organization (WHO), among others. Without a concerted effort on the parts of national and international governments, the problems of family violence will only grow worse.

One of the serious consequences of family violence for the larger society is the heavy burden the violence places on health care systems in both dollars and resources. Because families often do not seek medical help until the abused family member is seriously injured or ill, the medical intervention must be drastic, often requiring admittance to a hospital through an emergency room and a long stay in the hospital after that. Sometimes the injuries are so severe that the victim never fully recovers, requiring ongoing care and medical attention. For example, a child who suffers blunt force trauma to the head or who is vigorously shaken may have permanent brain damage resulting in a long-term coma. Likewise, an elderly person who is neglected may suffer dehydration, kidney damage, or a stroke and may not receive timely treatment, leading to premature admittance to a long-term care facility. A woman badly beaten by her intimate partner might need physical therapy to restore her mobility.

Furthermore, family violence puts a strain on mental health resources, since many victims of such violence suffer from post-traumatic stress disorder (PTSD) as a direct result of the assault. Children who are sexually molested by family members often must go through years of therapy to have any kind of a normal life. As a corollary, mental illness and addictions are documented as a risk factor for family violence. Often the reverse is also true: Family violence can actually cause mental illness and/or addiction to drugs or alcohol.

Treating injury and mental health problems is expensive not only for the family, but also for the nation as a whole, since a portion of a nation's wealth must be devoted to providing health care for its citizens, even in countries without nationalized medicine. In 2003, the CDC estimated that intimate partner violence costs $4.1 billion in direct medical and mental health care.

On a larger scale, countries that have widespread problems with the abuse of women at the hands of male relatives suffer from reduced capacity and gross domestic product. That is, in those countries where wives and daughters are regularly beaten, injured, or killed, the abused women are unable to contribute to the national economy through their work, consumption of goods, and the payment of taxes. The problem is so pervasive that it affects far more than the family itself—it damages the national economy. For example, as stated in the United Nations Population Fund (UNFPA) 2005 State of the World Population Fact Sheet, "Violence against women represents a drain on the economically productive workforce: Canada's national survey on violence against women reported that 30 per cent of battered wives had to cease regular activities due to the abuse, and 50 per cent of women had to take sick leave from work because of the harm sustained."

Perhaps the most worrisome consequence of family violence is the way that it perpetuates itself. A 2000 British Crime Survey conducted by the United Kingdom's Home Office and published in 2001 reports that "domestic violence has a higher rate of repeat victimization than any other type of crime." Further, a woman who is being abused by her husband is more likely to abuse her children. Children who are abused are at a high risk of becoming abusers themselves. The cycle, therefore, is intergenerational. Without significant public health intervention, the process cannot be broken.

Public health initiatives have the potential to educate, protect, and support the victims of family violence. Dr. Carmona noted in 2003 that US public health efforts are being committed to prevent family violence, and that "there is also a growing emphasis on strategies directed toward perpetrators and potential perpetrators to break the cycle of family violence." Once such public health initiative is the CDC's project, Domestic Violence Prevention Enhancement and Leadership Through Alliances (DELTA).

Likewise, international and national public health organizations have the resources to mount large-scale preventative programs that include raising public awareness, mitigating the shame felt by victims, encouraging potential abusers to get help, and training police to deal more effectively with family violence. For example, the World Health Organization writes on its web page "Prevention of Intimate Partner Violence and Sexual Violence" (2011) that WHO is stepping up efforts to address and treat the primary causes of family violence to stop the cycle. In addition, government public health programs in Europe, Asia, Africa, Australia, North America, and the Middle East are actively working toward eliminating family violence.

Educating the public about the many forms and degrees of family violence is a first step. The authors in *Global Viewpoints: Family Violence* document the extent of the problem and describe some of the faces of family violence: intimate partner violence; bride burning, dowry deaths, and honor killings; family violence directed toward children; and family violence directed toward the elderly.

Introduction

Family Violence and Intimate Partner Abuse

VIEWPOINT 1

Family Violence in the United States: An Overview

The National Center for Victims of Crime

Family violence, sometimes called domestic violence, is defined as abusive behavior perpetrated by one household member against another. According to the National Center for Victims of Crime, family violence can take forms such as physical, emotional, financial, or sexual abuse or assault. Most victims are women. The center asserts that victims suffer from a variety of symptoms similar to post-traumatic stress disorder and often stay in abusive situations because of fear or love. The National Center for Victims of Crime is an advocacy organization in the United States that helps victims of crime rebuild their lives.

As you read, consider the following questions:
1. What facilities were established in response to an increase of public consciousness regarding the treatment of women in the home?
2. What is post-traumatic stress disorder, according to the writers of the viewpoint?
3. How do many victims describe domestic violence perpetrators?

The National Center for Victims of Crime, "Domestic Violence," 2008. www.ncvc.org. Copyright © 2008 by the National Coalition Against Domestic Violence. All rights reserved. Reproduced by permission.

Family Violence

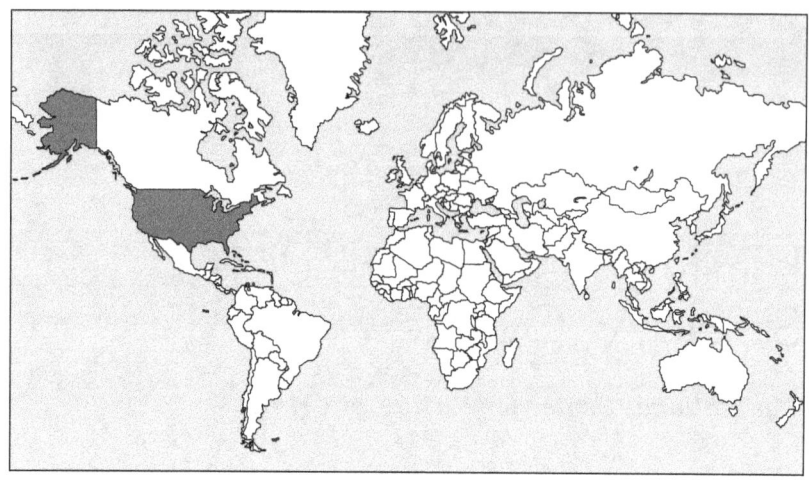

- One in every four women will experience domestic violence in her lifetime (Tjaden, Patricia et al., 2000), and females who are 20–24 years of age are at the greatest risk for intimate partner violence (US Department of Justice, 2006).

- In 2005, 389,100 women and 78,180 men were victimized by an intimate partner. These crimes accounted for 9 percent of all violent crime (Shannon M. Catalano, 2005).

- The majority (73%) of family violence victims are females: 84% were spousal abuse victims and 86% were victims at the hands of a boyfriend (US Department of Justice, 2005).

- A 2004 study found that women living in disadvantaged neighborhoods are more than twice as likely to be the victims of intimate partner violence than women in more affluent neighborhoods (Michael Benson et al., 2004).

- One study found that women who have experienced any type of personal violence (even when the last episode was 14 to 30 years ago) reported a greater number of chronic physical symptoms than those who have not been abused. The risk of suffering from six or more chronic physical symptoms increased with the number of forms of violence experienced (Christina Nicolaidis et al., 2004).

- In 2003, lesbians, gays, bisexuals, or transgender people experienced 6,523 incidents of domestic violence; 44% were men, 36% women and 2% transgender (National Coalition of Anti-Violence Programs, 2004).

The majority (73%) of family violence victims are females: 84% were spousal abuse victims and 86% were victims at the hands of a boyfriend.

Domestic Violence Defined

Domestic violence constitutes the willful intimidation, assault, battery, sexual assault or other abusive behavior perpetrated by one family member, household member, or intimate partner against another. In most state laws addressing domestic violence, the relationship necessary for a charge of domestic assault or abuse generally includes a spouse, former spouse, persons currently residing together or those that have within the previous year, or persons who share a common child. In addition, as of 2007, a majority of states provide some level of statutory protection for victims of dating violence....

An Overview of Domestic Violence

Domestic violence has been present since the early days of recorded history, and was even sanctioned in English common law as late as the early twentieth century. The women's movement in the 1970s, which brought to light the social plight of women and advocated for women's rights, fostered a growing concern over the treatment of women in the home. In response to this increase in public consciousness, shelters and resources were established to provide assistance to victims of domestic violence. The first shelter for battered women was established in 1974. Since then, hundreds of shelters and domestic violence programs throughout the United States provide emotional, financial, vocational, and sometimes legal assistance and support to domestic violence survivors and their children.

Domestic violence affects not only those abused, but witnesses, family members, coworkers, friends, and the community at large. Children who witness domestic violence are victims themselves and growing up amidst violence predisposes them to a multitude of social and physical problems. Constant exposure to violence in the home and abusive role models teach these children that violence is a normal way of life and places them at risk of becoming society's next generation of victims and abusers.

Constant exposure to violence in the home and abusive role models teach these children that violence is a normal way of life and places them at risk of becoming society's next generation of victims and abusers.

Dynamics of Domestic Violence

Domestic violence is about power and control. The abuser wants to dominate the victim/survivor and wants all the power in the relationship—and uses violence in order to establish and maintain authority and power. Perpetrators of domestic violence are usually not sick or deranged, but have learned abusive, manipulative techniques and behaviors that allow them to dominate and control others and obtain the responses they desire.

An abuser will often restrict a victim's outlets, forbidding the victim to maintain outside employment, friends, and family ties. This has an isolating effect, leaving victims with no support system and creating dependency. Abusers also limit a survivor's options by not allowing access to checking accounts, credit cards or other sources of money or financial independence.

Perpetrators of domestic violence may constantly criticize, belittle and humiliate their partners. Causing the victim to feel worthless, ugly, stupid and crazy does not allow for a survivor's healthy self-perception. Low self-esteem may contribute to victims feeling they deserve the abuse, affecting their ability to see themselves as worthy of better treatment.

Reactions of Domestic Violence Victims

Domestic violence victims are often exposed repeatedly to threats, violence, intimidation, and physical, emotional and psychological abuse. Constant, repeated exposure to violence has a profound effect on a victim's daily activities and functioning, thinking, interpersonal relationships, and sense of self. Some victims, because of the chronic nature of the violence, may develop post-traumatic stress disorder, a mental health disorder characterized by flashbacks, significant anxiety, depression and fatigue.

Other reactions a domestic violence survivor may experience include:

- Fear;
- Nightmares and sleep disturbances;
- Anxiety;
- Anger;
- Difficulty concentrating;
- Depression;
- Low self-esteem;

Family Violence

- Shame and embarrassment;
- Chronic physical complaints;
- Substance abuse;
- Social withdrawal;
- Feelings of helplessness and hopelessness;
- Self-blame;
- Numbness; and
- Hypervigilance (inability to relax, jumpiness).

Domestic violence victims will often blame their own behavior, rather than the violent actions of the abuser. Victims may try continually to alter their behavior and circumstances in order to please the abuser—believing that if they follow certain rules and make sure the abuser is happy, they will not be hurt. However, violence perpetrated by abusers is often self-driven and depends little on victims' actions or words.

Domestic violence victims may minimize the seriousness of incidents in order to cope, and not seek medical attention or assistance when needed. Victims, because they fear the perpetrator and may be ashamed of their situation, may be reluctant to disclose the abuse to family, friends, work, the authorities, or victim assistance professionals. As a consequence, they may suffer in silence and isolation.

Perpetrators of Domestic Violence

There is no typical domestic violence perpetrator, but psychologists have identified some common characteristics. Many abusers suffer from low self-esteem, and their sense of self and identity is tied to their partner. Therefore, if abusers feel they are somehow losing the victim, either through separation, divorce, emotional detachment, or pregnancy (fearing victims will replace love for them with love for a child), they will lash out. If victims "leave" through any of these methods, abusers feel they are losing power, control, and their self-identity. This is why it is particularly dangerous for victims during periods of separation or divorce from their partner. Abusers will often do anything to maintain control and keep the victim under control. This dynamic also makes escalating violence inevitable, as many victims must become emotionally unavailable, or must physically leave, in order to survive.

While the public may think of domestic violence abusers as out of control, crazy, and unpredictable, the contrary is most often true. Use of psychological, emotional, and physical abuse intermingled with periods of respite, love, and happiness are deliberate coercive tools used to generate submission. Abusers may violently assault, then minutes later offer words of regret. Many will buy gifts of flowers, candy and other presents in order to win favor and forgiveness. This creates a very confusing environment for victims. Abusers may say they will never harm their partners again, and promise to obtain help or counseling. Often, these promises are only made to prevent victims from leaving. Without getting help, the violence will most likely recur.

The violence used by abusers is controlled and manipulative. Victims often can predict exactly when violence will erupt. Many law enforcement officers have commented on their surprise at finding significant evidence of a violent incident, a harmed victim, and a composed perpetrator casually speaking with officers as if nothing occurred.

Finally, many victims describe domestic violence perpetrators as having a "Jekyll and Hyde" personality. Abusers often experience dramatic mood swings of highs and lows. They may be loving one minute, and spiteful and cruel the next. Abusers are frequently characterized by those outside the home as generous, caring, and good, and behave drastically differently in their home environment. Perpetrators of domestic violence are rarely violent to those outside of their domicile.

Why Victims May Stay

Very few individuals would become involved in a relationship they knew to be violent. Domestic violence has subtle origins. What starts out as love, courtship and concern, may turn into domination, forced adherence to rigid sex roles and obsessive jealousy. Victims are not masochists. They do not enjoy being hurt, abused, battered and controlled. Victims may stay with someone who is abusing them for various reasons, which include:

- Fear of the abuser;
- Love;
- Threats to harm the victim, loved ones or pets;
- Threats of suicide;
- Believing the abuser will take their children;
- Religious reasons;
- Believing the abuser will change;
- Self-blame;
- Limited financial options;
- Believing that violence is normal;
- Believing in the sanctity of marriage and the family;
- Limited housing options;
- Blaming the abuse on alcohol, financial pressures, or other outside factors;
- Low self-esteem;
- Fear of the unknown, of change;
- Isolation;
- Embarrassment and shame;

- Believing no one can help;
- Cultural beliefs;
- Denial; and
- Pressure from friends and family to stay.

References

Tjaden, Patricia & Thoennes, Nancy. National Institute of Justice and the Centers of Disease Control and Prevention, "Extent, Nature and Consequences of Intimate Partner Violence: Findings from the National Violence Against Women Survey." (2000). U.S. Department of Justice, Bureau of Justice Statistics, "Intimate Partner Violence in the United States," December 2006.

Catalano, Shannan M. "Criminal Victimization, 2005." (Washington, DC: Bureau of Justice Statistics, 2006).U.S. Department of Justice, Bureau of Justice Statistics, "Family Violence Statistics," June 2005.

Benson, Michael, and Fox, Greer. "When Violence Hits Home: How Economics and Neighborhood Play a Role," (Washington, DC: National Institutes of Justice, 2004).

Nicolaidis, Christina et al., "Violence, Mental Health and Physical Symptoms in an Academic Internal Medicine Practice," Journal of General Internal Medicine 19 (2004).

National Coalition of Anti-Violence Programs, "Lesbian, Gay, Bisexual and Transgender Domestic Violence: 2003 Supplement," (New York: National Coalition of Anti-Violence Programs, 2004).

Bibliography

Barnett, Ola W. and LaViolette, Alyce D. (1993). It Could Happen to Anyone. Newbury Park, CA: Sage Publications.

Bergen, Raquel Kennedy. (1998). Issues in Intimate Violence. Thousand Oaks, CA: Sage Publications.

Buzawa, E. and Buzawa, C. (1990). Domestic Violence: The Criminal Justice Response. Newbury Park, CA: Sage Publications.

Dutton, Donald G. (1995). The Batterer. New York, NY: Basic Books, Inc.

Mariani, Cliff. (1996). Domestic Violence Survival Guide. Flushing, NY: Looseleaf Law Publications, Inc.

Statman, Jan Berliner. (1990). The Battered Woman's Survival Guide: Breaking the Cycle. Dallas, TX: Taylor Publishing Company.

Walker, Lenore. (1979). The Battered Woman. New York, NY: Harper & Row Publishers, Inc.

White, Evelyn C. (1994). Chain, Chain, Change: For Black Women in Abusive Relationships. Seattle, WA: Seal Press.

VIEWPOINT

In Ireland, Women Bear the Brunt of Family Violence

Carol Hunt

Although some men claim otherwise, all of the data gathered in Ireland and worldwide provide evidence that women, far more often than men, are the victims of domestic violence, according to Carol Hunt. The only way the cycle of domestic violence can be broken is for children to be raised in homes where violence is not considered an acceptable form of behavior, she asserts. Because women who try to leave abusive situations are often assaulted, Hunt contends that more support must be offered to victims of domestic violence to increase the safety of both mothers and children. Hunt is a columnist for the Sunday Independent *in Ireland.*

As you read, consider the following questions:

1. In what percentage of cases do child abuse and partner abuse overlap, according to the viewpoint?
2. Of the women who have been murdered in Ireland in the preceding fourteen years, what percentage were killed by their partners or former partners?
3. What did the prosecution maintain in the Joe O'Reilly case?

Carol Hunt, "Women Do Bear Brunt of Domestic Violence," *The Sunday Independent* (Ireland), May 30, 2010. www.independent.ie. Copyright © 2010 by Independent Newspapers. All rights reserved. Reproduced with permission.

Family Violence

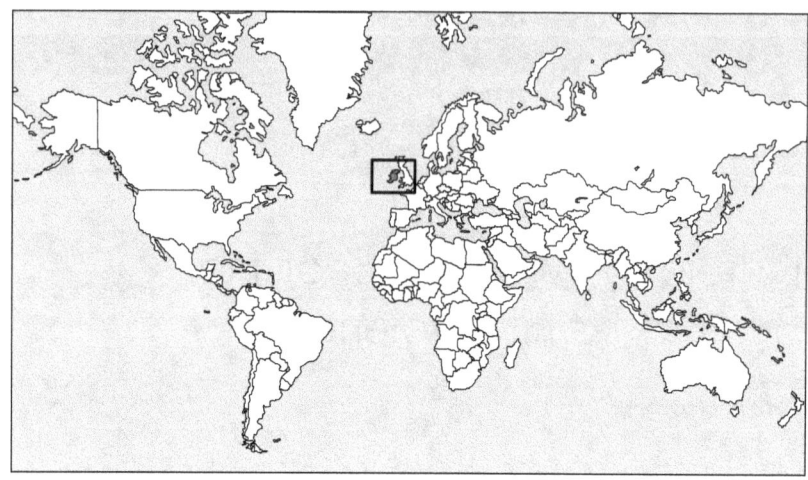

"Don't hit your sister." "But she..." The six-year-old is trying to explain that he was badly provoked. "Don't ever, ever hit a girl." I'm holding his outstretched arm away from his victim while he stutters at the injustice of it all. "Or anyone for that matter", I add. "But especially not girls, or anyone smaller than you. Just walk away instead."

I try to explain that boys grow up to have far greater strength than girls and that he should never get into the habit of hurting a girl physically—even if it is his older, annoying sister.

In their potential to do violent damage to each other, men and women are not equal. Fact. Which is probably why, in the report released last week [May 2010] by the HSE [Health Service Executive], "Practice document on domestic violence—a guide for working with children and families," the abused in a relationship is usually referred to as "the woman" or "women". I've since noticed that this has caused some outrage on various blogs commenting on the report.

One contributor to an *Irish Times* site commented: "It is simply not true that the 'vast majority' of adult victims of domestic violence are women." Another said that the statistics were skewed hugely towards the impression that most domestic abuse is perpetrated by males. "This is simply not the case," he added.

Really?

The Majority of Domestic Abuse Is Experienced by Women

Of course there are relationships, both heterosexual and homosexual, where men are violently abused, but overwhelmingly the vast bulk of domestic abuse in our society is experienced by women and perpetrated by men, and putting this fact down in black and white should not immediately label me a man-hating feminist with an agenda.

Nor should it imply that I am minimising the suffering of men who are caught up in abusive situations.

> *[Irish] women were more than twice as likely as men to experience severe physical abuse, nearly three times as likely to suffer severe emotional abuse, and 10 times more likely to require a stay in hospital after . . . abuse.*

Neither can it be interpreted as a belief that most men have the potential to become violent thugs.

But the bare truth of the matter is that women suffer from violence in the home more than men. Fact.

All the documentation collated both in Ireland and worldwide shows this to be true—(the 2005 ESRI [Economic and Social Research Institute]/National Crime Council report showed that women were more than twice as likely as men to experience severe physical abuse, nearly three times as likely to suffer severe emotional abuse, and 10 times more likely to require a stay in hospital after the experience of abuse)—regardless of the attempts of a small, but dangerous (I'll get back to this) minority to deny this.

Children Should Not Be Raised in Violence

Of course, the most effective way to ensure that your children grow up knowing that violence is not acceptable is if they live in a home where fists are never raised. It is estimated that domestic abuse is present in about a fifth of Irish families. Child abuse and partner violence are estimated to overlap in 40 per cent to 50 per cent of cases. That's a lot of damaged kids.

And as [chief executive officer] Fergus Finlay of Barnardo's [an Irish charity] said in a speech given some years ago: "An attack on a mother, or systematic violence against a mother, can undermine the relationship between her and her children. Children who struggle to understand violence in their homes can often be as willing to blame the victim as they are reluctant to blame the perpetrator."

Women who leave—or even express the wish to leave— their partners are five times more likely to be assaulted than those who decide to stay.

And children aren't the only ones. There still seems to be a prevailing view in some circles that women who stay in violent relationships are professional victims, somehow colluding in their own abuse, because—as has been pointed out to me many times—if they really wanted to leave, they would. Oh, if only things were so simple.

Two years ago [2008] I wrote an article in [the *Independent*] detailing the reasons why many women (and some men) make the choice to remain in the family home with an abusive partner rather than leave. Chief among them was the sobering fact that women who leave—or even express the wish to leave—their partners are five times more likely to be assaulted than those who decide to stay.

Intimate Partner Abuse in Ireland

- 47% of men who physically abuse their spouses do so at least 3 times per year.

- 1 in 7 women in Ireland experience severe domestic violence.

- 1 in 17 men in Ireland experience severe domestic abuse.

- 76% of women who have left abusive intimate partners suffer from continued violence from their former partners.

- 90% of domestic abuse offenders in 2003 were male.

- Before reporting abuse to the police, a woman will have been assaulted on average 35 times by her intimate partner.

Based on data from Women's Aid, "National and International Statistics," 2010. www.womensaid.ie.

Women in Danger of Their Lives

In cases where convictions have been secured, more than half of the women murdered in Ireland over the past 14 years were killed by their partner or former partner, many when they were at the point of leaving the relationship, or just after. Many of those murdered had a history of domestic violence. (In contrast, the vast majority of men murdered are killed by other men, in a variety of circumstances.)

In recognition of the danger that many women face when they try to leave a violent home, the HSE guidelines released last week recommend that social workers should not immediately encourage an abused woman to leave her situation in case this provokes a "catastrophic event".

Instead, she should receive support to enable her to increase her safety and that of her children.

Also, the guidelines recommend implementing a violence-prevention programme targeted at children or those who influence them, noting: "Such early intervention has the potential to shape the attitude, knowledge and behaviour of children while they are more open to positive influences."

And, of course, the earliest influences on children are their parents—fathers inculcating respect for women in their sons have a very important role here.

Difficulty in Changing Behaviors

There are many other positive and progressive suggestions within this document, but the million-dollar question is: how can these recommendations be put into practice in our current economic climate? Who's going to pay for the extra social workers needed? And for the training that the current ones will require? Most groups working in this very area have had their budgets slashed.

This is not the only problem facing groups who work with victims of domestic violence. Increasingly, a small but very vocal minority of individuals and groups insinuate that by banging on about female victims of domestic abuse we are collectively demonising men—who, they allege, suffer just as much violence at the hands of women (despite the fact that no evidence, in Ireland or elsewhere, supports this view).

Then there is the increasingly held belief—again asserted by these self-same groups—that men whose partners leave them (or vice versa) are invariably "screwed" if they go to court and that the entire legal system in Ireland is prejudiced in favour of women. Yet the Family Law Reporting Pilot Project which reported to the Courts Service in 2007 saw "no evidence of systematic bias against fathers or anyone else in the courts". Even so, many vulnerable men in relationships that are breaking down choose not to believe this.

The prosecution in the Joe O'Reilly case[1] maintained that O'Reilly "got rid" of his wife partly because he was afraid of losing custody of their children in any separation proceedings. O'Reilly had obviously bought into the myth that men are "screwed" if they go to court.

Who knows how many of the 162 women murdered in Ireland since 1996 met their deaths precisely because of these reasons? This misinformation can be deadly.

Organisations that provide help and support to men in times of crisis make a very valuable contribution to our society. But the fact that some seem able to do so only by casting themselves as the "new oppressed", and denigrating and denying the suffering of women at the hands of men, is both tragic and irresponsible.

---

1. A 2007 trial in which Irishman Joe O'Reilly was convicted of murdering his wife in 2004.

VIEWPOINT 3

In Australia, Some Men Are Abused by Their Intimate Partners

Andrea Mayes

In Australia, evidence suggests that as many as one in three victims of domestic violence is a man. Most men fail to report abuse from their intimate partners due to shame, according to Andrea Mayes. Emotional abuse is the most common form the violence takes. Men who have tried to take advantage of social services to help victims of domestic violence find little support or help. Many feel that they are not believed. Mayes notes that some believe the attention given to women victims of abuse has taken away attention that ought to be directed toward male victims. Mayes is a journalist who writes for the West Australian newspaper.

As you read, consider the following questions:

1. Why is it difficult to get a true understanding of the prevalence of domestic violence against men in Australia?
2. Who is Elizabeth Celi, and what is her specialty?
3. For how long did Alan Edwards lose the parenting role he had previously enjoyed with his son?

Andrea Mayes, "Men Can Be Victims Too," *West Australian* (Perth), May 22, 2010. Copyright © 2010 by Andrea Mayes. All rights reserved. Reproduced by permission.

Family Violence and Intimate Partner Abuse

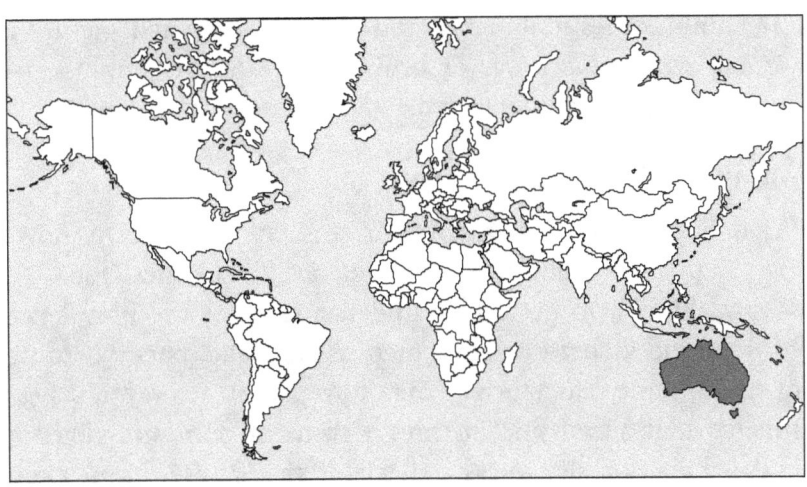

"I was hit, I was punched, I was head-butted, I was bruised. I felt trapped, physically and emotionally, and isolated from my friends and family. I felt such a sense of shame that this was happening to me."

This quote from a victim of domestic violence is sadly typical of those suffering at the hands of abusive partners except in one crucial respect. The victim in this instance is male.

Alan Edwards (not his real name) spent three years in an abusive relationship with the mother of his young son before seeking help.

He was verbally and physically abused in front of his son, had his front door kicked down and felt pushed to his emotional limit.

"I'm six foot one and I weigh 90kg [198 lbs.], and I would rather be punched in the face by a man than be shamed in this way by a woman," he said. "You can get over the physical damage but the emotional abuse is so much harder. People don't even recognise that it's there for a start.

The shame comes from a lack of support. If people are supporting and validating me, the shame doesn't land. Nobody told me that I was right and she was wrong. The shame can't be relieved, so it doesn't go away."

Think domestic violence and chances are you'll picture a woman with a black eye or bruising, one of the graphic images used in government media campaigns of recent years.

Men Can Be Victims, Too

What these very successful campaigns fail to mention, however, is that the victims of such violence can be men, too.

It's difficult to get a true understanding of the prevalence of domestic violence against men in Australia, partly because of the extreme reluctance of men to report it. However, it's estimated that about one in three victims of domestic violence in Australia is male, and the effects of such abuse on men can be just as devastating as on women.

The experience of male victims is the subject of a groundbreaking new study by researchers at Edith Cowan University that will be released next week [May 2010].

Believed to be the first report in Australia to look in depth at men's experiences of domestic violence, the *Intimate Partner Abuse of Men* study was commissioned by the Men's Advisory Network and interviewed male victims, family members who had witnessed the effect of the abuse, and service providers.

It's estimated that about one in three victims of domestic violence in Australia is male.

It found that men suffered from a similar range of abuse as women, from physical, verbal and sexual to psychological, financial and social isolation.

Abuse against the person ranged from punching, biting, scratching, spitting and the throwing of objects at men, to the spiking of their drinks, the report found.

Men reported being repeatedly put down and humiliated, being forced to submit to sex against their will, having their financial affairs controlled and being cut off from their family and friends. The report also identified the new category of legal administrative abuse, where women use things such as violence restraining orders inappropriately to deliberately hurt their partners.

Emotional Abuse Is Most Common

Psychologist Elizabeth Celi, who specialises in men's health, says domestic violence against men often takes the form of emotional abuse, making it harder to detect than physical abuse.

She says people often assume that men don't feel hurt by emotional abuse because they don't talk about it, yet their sense of shame, failure and self-doubt can be more acute than that of female victims.

Men's health is intricately wrapped up in men's identity, she says. Female perpetrators can attack him physically, and worse yet, attack his role as a father, a worker and a man in his own right. So the emotional impact on a man's self-confidence and subsequent mental health problems can be grossly underestimated.

Just because he doesn't verbalise it doesn't mean he doesn't feel it.

Greg Andresen, a spokesman for the One in Three campaign, which aims to raise public awareness of family violence against men, says the popular belief that men are tough and can look after themselves physically was backed up by statistics that showed more women than men suffered from physical abuse in relationships.

Men can become suicidal when the abuse is at its most severe.

But often the worse damage to men comes from the emotional and psychological abuse, he says. "Having your life controlled in such a way that you're utterly powerless, not being allowed to see your friends and family and not having money to spend—these sort of impacts are the same whether you're a burly six-foot bloke or a petite woman."

Dr Celi says men can become suicidal when the abuse is at its most severe.

Their diminished self-worth can also see them withdraw from their social circles, withdraw from their life and develop destructive behaviours like increased alcohol use, she said.

Alan Edwards was forced to move to a different town, away from his young son, to escape the abuse.

"I ended up having to move out and let go of my baby. And because I was a hands-on parent, that was like a mother giving up her child," he says.

"I had to let go of my baby when he was three years old, and took me another three or four years before I got him back on a 50–50 (shared care) basis."

The report found men were reluctant to report abuse for a number of reasons, all of them familiar to Mr Edwards, including shame and embarrassment and fear of being judged as weak.

Others didn't want to report it for fear of what would happen to their children.

Many were also afraid they would not be believed, would not be helped or would be blamed for the abuse which is what happened to some victims. Others had their experiences dismissed or played down.

"I spoke to everybody—counsellors, psychologists, lawyers, police—everybody just went oh gee, if she's that bad, get away from there," one man told researchers.

Nowhere to Turn

Yet despite the evidence of domestic violence against men, and despite the plethora of services for female victims of abuse, there is almost nowhere for a male victim to turn.

Men who had tried to use existing services such as helplines, GPs [general practitioners] and police, had found them unhelpful and even hostile towards men, the report found.

Mr Edwards says police laughed at him and other services had no way of helping him.

"The police at the counter actually sniggered at me and gave each other knowing looks," he said.

"There was nowhere for me to go and that was one of the biggest problems.

Not only was I isolated on a country farm with this violent person, when I went to seek services there was very little they could do for me and, even if they wanted to, there was very little understanding of how it is for men. And it's different for men than it is for women."

ECU [Edith Cowan University] researcher Alfred Allan said there were no services specifically for men as victims of domestic violence.

"We found that when men finally did pluck up the courage to report their abuse, there was nowhere for them to turn or they felt they simply were not believed," Professor Allan said.

A lot of the service providers we interviewed felt really sorry for the men and wanted to help them but simply could not because they didn't have the facilities or experience.

Community Services Minister Robyn McSweeney says the support services offered to domestic violence victims are not gender specific and can therefore be accessed by anyone presenting as a victim or perpetrator of family and domestic violence.

She says women and children experience violence at much greater rates than men do and although male victims could use crisis care and helplines, the majority of male callers present as perpetrators of violence seeking help to change their behaviour.

Similarly, government and media campaigns targeting women and children as victims of domestic violence are most often designed to help reduce the high rates at which the most vulnerable within our community experience violence within an intimate or family relationship.

Ironically, the success of such media campaigns may have contributed to the problems men face getting help.

A Mistaken Impression

Dr Celi believes these campaigns have helped create the impression that only men can be perpetrators and only women can be victims.

"The much-needed work in recent decades in raising awareness for female victims has created the unfortunate and ridiculous side effect of making all men out to be potential perpetrators and erroneously viewing them with caution," Dr Celi says.

"Male victims are then approached with negative judgments and far less compassion and empathy than female victims which is simply inequitable. We need to remember that any forms of abuse and violence against anyone, regardless of gender, are simply unacceptable."

Men's Advisory Network executive officer Gary Bryant backs the report's recommendations for government-funded public awareness campaigns, for publicly funded services for male victims, and for training for people working in health and welfare to help them assist male victims.

"We're not trying to say that men are not the perpetrators of domestic violence, but what we are saying is that men can be victims too and that they need appropriate support services and systems," he says.

Mr Edwards was one of the lucky ones.

Having had previous professional experience in the area of men's health, he was eventually able to get some support from former colleagues.

"They ended up validating me, which was at least enough for me to hold my own, and helped me see that I had to get out," he says.

For three years he lost the hands-on parenting role he had previously enjoyed with his son, but eventually won a Family Court [of Australia] order giving him shared custody.

"'Now I've got a court order she seems to understand and things have got better," he says.

"The emotional impact on a man's self-confidence and subsequent mental health problems can be grossly underestimated."

VIEWPOINT 4

In Nigeria, Family Violence Affects Many Women

IRIN

IRIN writes that many Nigerian women are victims of family violence. Amnesty International, an organization dedicated to ending the abuse of human rights, estimates that up to two-thirds of women in the Lagos communities are victims of physical and psychological abuse at the hands of their family members. Amnesty International is urging the government of President Olusegun Obasanjo to monitor the familial violence against Nigerian women and to take legislative action to end the violence. IRIN is an award-winning humanitarian news and analysis service that covers often underreported parts of the world.

As you read, consider the following questions:

1. According to Amnesty, the abuses against Nigerian women were often carried out by whom?
2. According to the article, does the justice system fail to offer protection to women who have suffered from family violence?
3. As stated in the article, what is "explicitly excluded from the definition of rape and is therefore not a crime"?

IRIN, "Nigeria: Women Getting No Protection Against High Levels of Abuse, Says Amnesty," May 31, 2005. Copyright © 2005 by IRIN. All rights reserved. Reproduced by permission.

Family Violence and Intimate Partner Abuse

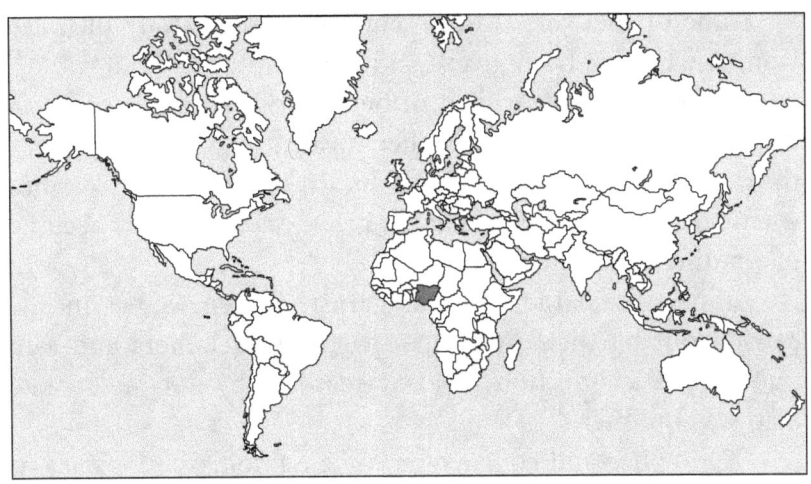

Lagos, 31 May 2005 (IRIN)—Up to two-thirds of women in and around Nigeria's biggest city Lagos have suffered some form of abuse at the hands of family members sometimes simply for not having dinner on the table, Amnesty International said on Tuesday as it urged the government to do more to help them.

In a report entitled "Nigeria: Unheard Voices", the human rights group said the widespread gender violence was enveloped by silence and that state authorities did nothing to stop the attacks happening, in some cases even going so far as to condone them.

"On a daily basis, Nigerian women are beaten, raped and even murdered by members of their family for supposed transgressions, which can range from not having meals ready on time to visiting family members without their husband's permission," said Stephane Mikala, deputy director of Amnesty's Africa Programme.

Amnesty said there were no official statistics but estimated that up to two-thirds of women in certain communities in Lagos State had been the victims of physical, sexual or psychological violence in the family.

Some of the worst cases mentioned in the study included women who had been given 'acid baths'.

"Ronke from Lagos died of her injuries after she had acid thrown over her allegedly by her husband's younger brother," the report said. "Her husband had died from a stroke but when she attended his funeral . . . she was apparently accused of wanting to kill him."

Amnesty said that abuses against women were typically carried out by their husbands, partners or fathers and said this familial connection was one reason why not much state help was on offer.

"The police and courts often dismiss domestic violence as a family matter and refuse to investigate or press charges," said Itoro Eze-Anaba of the Lagos-based Legal Defence and Assistance Project (LEDAP), which helped research the study.

Abuses against women were typically carried out by their husbands, partners or fathers and said this familial connection was one reason why not much state help was on offer.

Lack of Justice

Even when the attacker is not related to the victim, justice was not forthcoming, Amnesty said.

"It was Folake who was jailed after she accused a man of rape," the report recounted.

"She said her employer's husband had forced her into his bedroom and made her watch a violent videotape before forcing her to have sex. A medical examination supported her allegation. Yet she was the one brought to court, charged with slander for making the accusation and remanded in prison until her family could raise the bail money."

According to Amnesty International, the situation in Lagos is reflective of the level of domestic violence across Africa's most populous country of more than 126 million people.

Gender-Based Violence in Tanzania

Gender-based violence (GBV) is a grave reality in the lives of many women in Tanzania. It results from gender norms and social and economic inequities that give privilege to men over women. There is a mounting recognition in Tanzania of gender discrimination and gender equity in different facets of life. This awakening includes a growing acknowledgement of how prevalent gender-based violence is and the ways and extent to which it harms not only women and girls but also men and boys and, furthermore, the country's developing economy and health and social welfare systems. . . .

[M]any forms of gender-based violence, including intimate partner violence and rape, are seen as normal and are met with acceptance by both men and women. . . . Women and girls are also frequently blamed for causing or provoking gender-based violence. . . .

On the other hand, at the policy level, there are signs of support to actively address GBV. For example, President [Jakaya] Kikwete has publicly stated that gender-based violence should be included as one of the [United Nations] Millennium Development Goals. . . .

Tanzanian law has shown some progress in preventing and punishing GBV crimes. For example, the Sexual Offences Special Provisions Act of 1998 poses harsh penalties for perpetrators of sexual violence. However, gaps remain in the legal system. In particular, domestic violence is only minimally and vaguely addressed in The Law of Marriage Act—although without specified penalties—and through the penal codes on general violence and assault. There is no law against domestic violence, specifically.

Myra Betron, Gender-Based Violence in Tanzania: An Assessment of Policies, Services, and Promising Interventions, *USAID Health Policy Initiative, November 2008. www.usaid.gov.*

The report acknowledged that some legal reforms were slowly being enacted. It cited a federal Violence Against Women Bill that recently received its first reading in the National Assembly, and the fact that local authorities in Lagos State were currently mulling the first state-level bill on violence in the family.

"Yet massive levels of family violence remain untouched by these developments," Amnesty said. "In most cases, the criminal justice system fails to offer protection, justice or redress to women who have been subjected to violence in the home."

And marital rape is explicitly excluded from the definition of rape and is therefore not a crime, the rights group said.

Discriminating Against Women

It also pointed out that where laws do exist, their provisions are often discriminatory to women.

For instance, Amnesty said, the punishment prescribed by the Nigerian criminal code for indecent assault against a man is three years imprisonment, while the punishment for the same offence committed against a woman is only two years.

And marital rape is explicitly excluded from the definition of rape and is therefore not a crime, the rights group said.

In its recommendations, Amnesty called on the government of President Olusegun Obasanjo to monitor violence against women in the home more closely, take legislative action to stem it, end judicial discrimination against women and take measures to challenge the social prejudices that encourage the gender violence.

VIEWPOINT 5

In Vietnam, Many Women Are Abused by Their Partners

General Statistics Office of Vietnam

A 2010 study undertaken by the government of Vietnam and the United Nations revealed that 34 percent of ever-married women have experienced physical abuse at the hands of their husbands. The problem remains largely unexplored, since women are reluctant to report the violence or believe that such violence is normal in relationships. In addition, many children are also abused by their mother's husband or partner. The General Statistics Office of Vietnam is the governmental agency charged with the compilation and analysis of all statistics in the country.

As you read, consider the following questions:

1. By whom are Vietnamese women most likely to be abused?
2. What ethnic group has a reported lifetime prevalence rate of domestic violence of 8 percent? What ethnic group reports a rate of 36 percent?
3. What percentage of women with children under fifteen years of age reported that their children have been physically abused by their husbands?

General Statistics Office of Vietnam, "New Study Shows High Prevalence of Domestic Violence in Vietnam," *National Study on Domestic Violence Against Women in Vietnam*, November 25, 2010. www.dso.govvn/defaul_en.aspx?tabid=487&ItemID=10693. Copyright © 2010 by General Statistic Office of Vietnam. All rights reserved. Reproduced with permission.

51

Family Violence

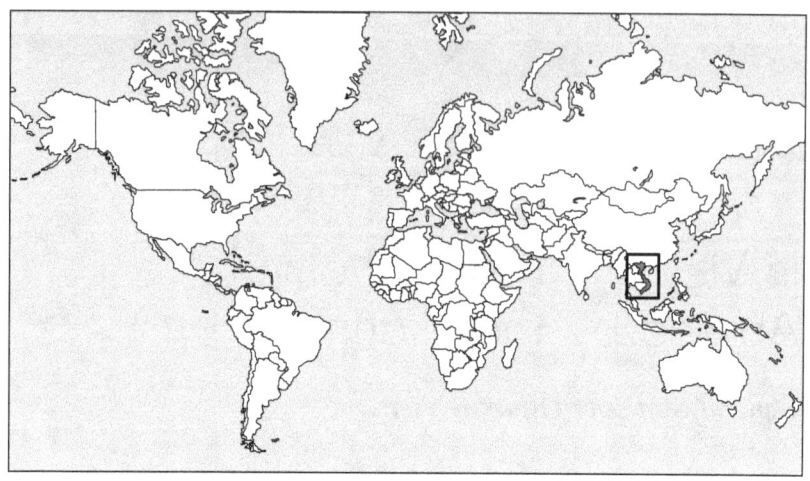

One in three, or 34 percent, of ever-married women report that they have suffered physical or sexual violence from their husbands at some time in their lives, according to the *National Study on Domestic Violence Against Women in Viet Nam*, launched today [November 25, 2010] by the Government of Viet Nam and the United Nations. Ever-married women who are *currently* experiencing either of these two types of violence amount to 9 percent.

When all three main types of partner violence—physical, sexual and emotional—are considered, more than half (58 percent) of Vietnamese women report experiencing at least one type of domestic violence in their lifetime. The study findings also show that women are three times more likely to be abused by a husband than by any other person.

"For the first time, a study seeks to obtain detailed information nationwide about the prevalence, frequencies and types of violence against women, looking at the health outcomes of domestic violence, the factors that may protect or put women at risk of domestic violence and showing coping strategies and services that women use to deal with domestic violence," explained Tran Thi Hang, Deputy General Director of GSO [General Statistics Office].

The Home Can Be Unsafe for Women

New data from the study highlight the fact that most women in Viet Nam are potentially at risk of domestic violence at some point in their lives. In some regions of the country, the home is not a safe place for four out of ten women. In the South East region, for example, 42 percent of women report having experienced physical or sexual violence by their husbands at some time. However, while there are regional variations, greater differences are evident between different ethnic groups, with reported lifetime prevalence rates of domestic violence ranging from 8 percent (H'Mong) to 36 percent (Kinh).

"Although domestic violence is widespread, the problem is very much hidden," said Ms. Henrica A.F.M. Jansen, the lead researcher of the study. "Besides the stigma and shame causing women to remain silent, many women think that violence in relationships is 'normal' and that women should tolerate and endure what is happening to them for the sake of family harmony." In fact, one in two women said that before the survey interviews, they had never told anyone about instances of violence by their husbands.

In some regions of [Viet Nam], the home is not a safe place for four out of ten women.

"This report highlights the urgency of breaking the silence," stressed Jean Marc Olive, WHO [World Health Organization] Representative in Viet Nam. "All of us owe it to the women who suffer from domestic violence, and the women who took part in this survey, to step up, speak out, and end domestic violence."

The Consequences of Family Violence

It is clear that domestic violence has serious consequences on both the physical and mental health of women. In Viet Nam,

Addressing Intimate Partner Violence in Vietnam

Married women in rural Vietnam are heavily exposed to all forms of serious abuse repeatedly over time from their husbands or male partners. This poses a serious threat not only to the women's health but also to their children and other family members and constitutes a serious violation of women's rights. There is an urgent need for effective support, counselling and treatment of violence victims where health care staff has a role to play as they are to observe professional secrecy and are relatively easy to access. Screening procedures for early detection is of utmost importance and health care staff at all levels are in need of training in how to address victimised women and their partners. Staff at health centres and health posts need counselling skills and training in how to pose sensitive questions on violence to feel confident in handling complicated situations. Hospital-based staff could form a point of referral for treatment and counselling. Locally elected representatives organised in women's unions, people's committees, youth unions and local reconciliation groups could form support groups for counselling. Media have a role to play in creating a debate on this topic and the national level needs to be strict on rules and regulations to be updated and followed. Explicit criminalisation of marital rape would send out an important signal on the unacceptability of the use of force within the family.

Nguyen Dang Vung, Per-Olof Ostergren, and Gunilla Krantz, "Intimate Partner Violence Against Women in Rural Vietnam – Different Socio-Demographic Factors Are Associated with Different Forms of Violence: Need for New Intervention Guidelines?" BMC Public Health, *2008. www.biomedcentral.com.*

one in four women who were physically or sexually abused by their husbands reported suffering physical injuries, and more than half of them reported being injured multiple times. Compared to women who have never been abused, those who have experienced partner violence are almost two times more likely to report poor health and physical problems, and three times more likely to have ever thought of suicide.

Pregnant women are also at risk. According to the report, about 5 percent of women who had been pregnant reported being beaten during pregnancy. In almost all of these cases, the women had been abused by the father of the unborn child.

About 5 percent of women who had been pregnant reported being beaten during pregnancy. In almost all of these cases, the women had been abused by the father of the unborn child.

Although domestic violence takes a heavy toll on women, children are also victims. Almost one in four women with children under 15 years of age reported that their children have been abused physically by their husbands. The study indicates that domestic violence poses serious risks for the well-being of the children. For example, the report shows that children living in a household where their mother was abused by her husband were more likely to have behavioral problems compared to other children.

"Women who have been abused have more chances to have a husband whose mother was beaten or who was himself beaten when he was a child. The childhood experience of the husband is an important risk factor with respect to him being a perpetrator later in life," said Jansen. This reinforces the idea that violence is a learned behavior.

VIEWPOINT 6

In Scotland, Many Victims of Family Violence Remain Silent

Tanya Thompson

Middle-class Scottish women are unlikely to report spousal abuse because of fear they will be stigmatized, reports Tanya Thompson. Those who have higher social standing are keenly aware of what people will think of them. Nevertheless, domestic violence rates are going up quickly. The Scottish government is funding a program to address the problem, although some believe more needs to be done to protect women since as few as 10 to 15 percent of abuse cases are identified as such in hospitals. Thompson is the correspondent for Social Affairs for the Scotsman.

As you read, consider the following questions:

1. Figures reveal that a victim of domestic violence will endure how many incidents of abuse before telling the police?
2. How much money in British pounds and American dollars does the Scottish government plan on spending to address violence against women and domestic abuse?
3. In 2007–2008, how many incidents of domestic abuse did police record in Scotland? How does this figure compare with the incidents of domestic abuse in 2004–2005?

Tanya Thompson, "Hope for 'Silent' Middle-Class Abuse Victims," *The Scotsman*, February 24, 2009. Copyright © 2009 by *The Scotsman*. All rights reserved. Reproduced by permission.

Family Violence and Intimate Partner Abuse

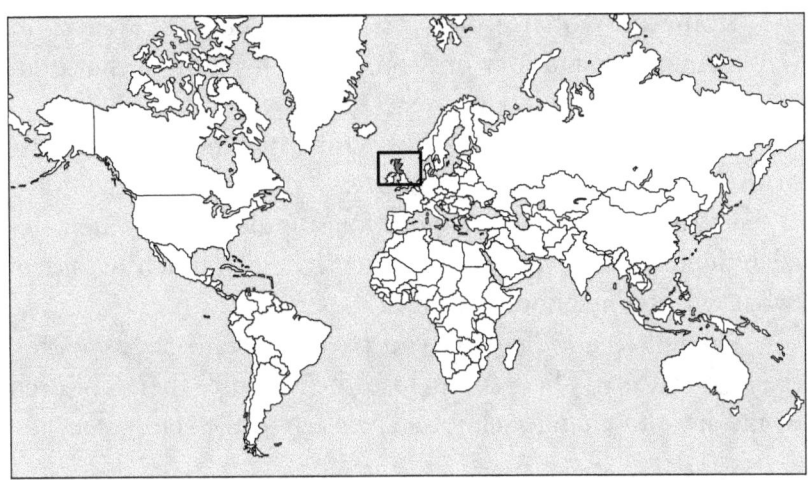

Scotland's largest health board has launched an early-intervention scheme to crack down on domestic violence amid fears that middle-class women are failing to report abuse.

In the first programme of its kind in Scotland, NHS [National Health Service] Greater Glasgow and Clyde is training key staff in hospitals and health centres to pinpoint warning signs.

The project comes as figures reveal that a victim will typically withstand 35 incidents of domestic violence before telling the police.

Last night [in February 2009], academics warned middle-class women often refused to seek help because of the stigma associated with the crime. And they cited doctors, church ministers and sheriffs as some of the perpetrators of abuse.

Family Violence Occurs in All Classes

Sandra Brown, a leading child-protection expert, said affluent women were embarrassed to admit to family and friends they had been attacked.

She said: "We have personally come across sheriffs' wives and GPs' [general practitioners'] children who have been victims of abuse.

"Domestic violence does not respect class. It weaves its way through the tapestry of Scottish life. It's a myth that it affects only working-class women."

Mrs Brown said that many victims hid the truth because of their family's standing in society.

She said: "There is a stigma for middle-class women. It's all hidden behind the net curtains. It's very much a case of 'what will the neighbours think?'.

"If you are a GP's wife, you have a certain status within the community. They could lose their home, their children would have to change schools. Their economic status goes."

Family Violence Is on the Rise

Recent figures show a marked rise in the number of reported cases of domestic violence in Scotland.

Statistics released in November [2008] showed an increase of almost 14 per cent in four years. Those most at risk of violence are women aged 31 to 35.

Dr Linda de Caestecker, NHS Greater Glasgow and Clyde's director of public health, said it would be dangerous to presume that middle-class women could not be victims of extreme violence.

And she said specially trained health professionals would discreetly ask patients whether they needed help to escape a violent partner, so that victims would not fall through the net.

[In Scotland] statistics released in November [2008] showed an increase [of domestic violence] of almost 14 per cent in four years.

The scheme, which has already been introduced in maternity units, is expected to be up and running within the year.

Staff will ask patients about their experience of domestic abuse and other gender-based violence, while speaking to them regarding other health issues.

Dr de Caestecker said: "The scale of the problem is worrying and the fact that so many people—in particular women—suffer abuse for so long without feeling able to tell anyone about it must be tackled.

"That, on average, a woman will withstand 35 incidents of domestic violence before reporting tells us just how important it is to create more opportunities for professional and sensitive early intervention.

"This highly ambitious step by the board will create a discreet opportunity for patients to raise domestic abuse with trained health professionals at an earlier stage than they might otherwise have felt able to."

New Training for Health Care Professionals

Staff in GP services, health visitors and mental health services will receive the specialist training to increase the early intervention approach rapidly.

If a victim does report domestic abuse, the aim is to make an assessment of her situation and offer support.

A spokeswoman for the board said the majority of women its members had spoken to were comfortable about being questioned.

The Scottish Government recently announced funding of nearly GBP 44 million [about $220 million] to address violence against women and domestic abuse—more than double the investment in 2005–8.

But Dr Mairead Tagg, a psychologist who works with victims of domestic abuse, said more needed to be done to protect women. She described services for women in Scotland as "hit and miss" and said research had shown that, in hospitals, only 10 to 15 per cent of domestic abuse was picked up.

She warned that the true tally was unknown, because many women suffered in silence for years. She said: "Domestic abuse

Family Violence

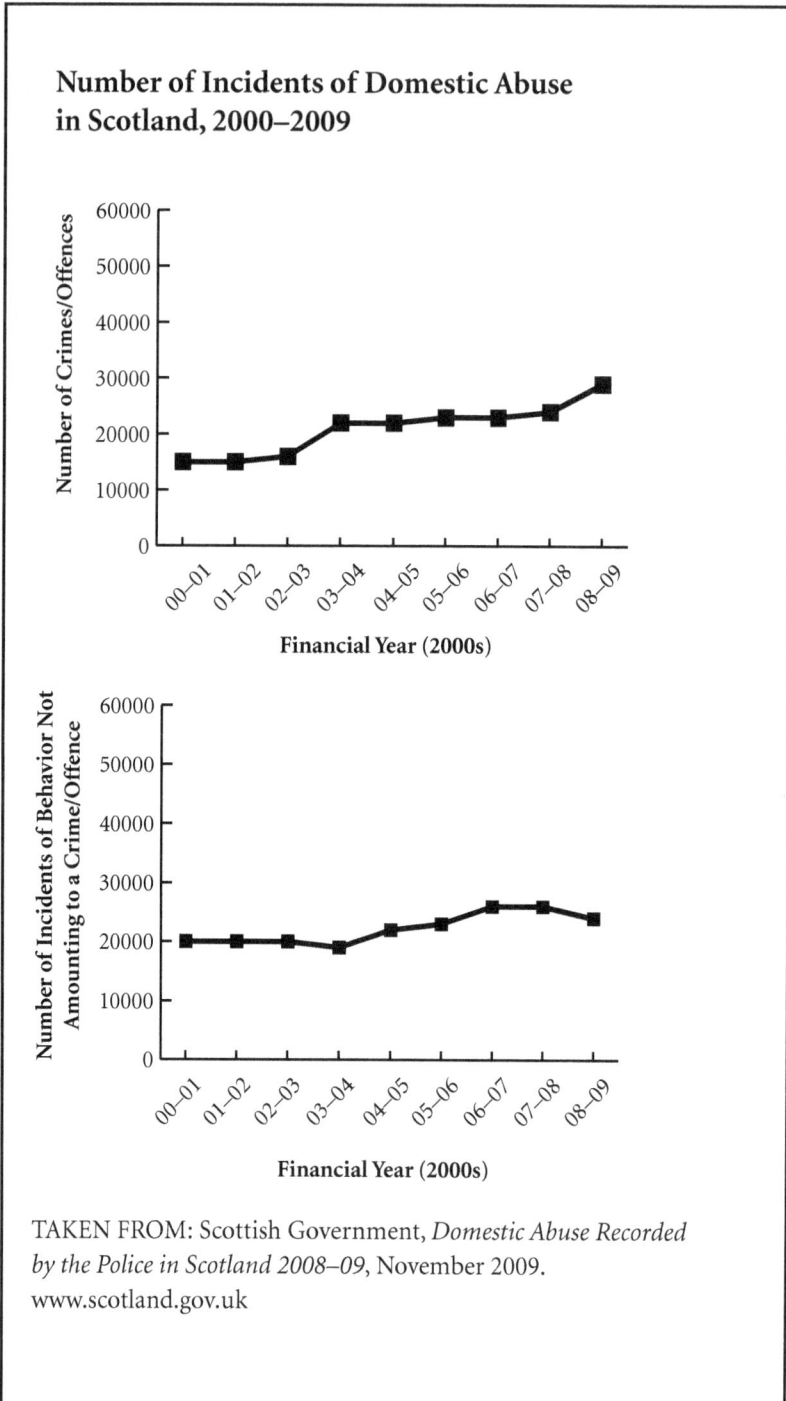

TAKEN FROM: Scottish Government, *Domestic Abuse Recorded by the Police in Scotland 2008–09*, November 2009. www.scotland.gov.uk

happens across the social spectrum. We've worked with the wives of ministers ... and doctors' wives, a psychiatrist's wife. Unless staff are well-trained in A&E [accident and emergency], it will not be picked up." ...

A Case Study in Family Violence

Just six weeks into her marriage Mary (not her real name) knew her life was in danger, but it took 14 years of domestic violence before she finally made the break.

To the outside world, all was well. Neighbours knew nothing of the regular beatings and she kept up the pretence of "playing happy families" with her husband and three children.

Regarded as a pillar of the community, her involvement in church groups and the setting up of a family centre for underprivileged children in Glasgow belied what was going on in her own home. She said: "I was involved in so many social projects, helping people, and yet no one realised what was happening.

"You wear a mask and people don't see beyond that. It was a case of keeping up appearances.

"The black eyes were pretty obvious, so I just stopped visiting my family until the bruises had healed."

With a steady job working for a local authority, her husband was regarded as a loving family man and she admits she helped maintain that façade for too long.

Mary, 57, is quick to point out that domestic violence affects women of all social classes and backgrounds. Time and again at counselling sessions and self-help groups, she has confided in all kinds of women suffering the same kind of abuse.

"It's not just poor people that domestic violence affects. Domestic abuse is not all about people living in the East End of Glasgow, in poverty. It covers every class."

Bruised from head to foot with a black eye and broken nose, there were only so many times she could lie to friends and say she had fallen down the stairs. Only so many times she could say she had suffered another "accident".

But it was the devastating impact on her three children who had witnessed the abuse that forced her to act.

"I lived in total fear. I decided one night that I had to leave. I went to a refuge with the kids.

"It took 14 years before I finally got out."

In the [United Kingdom] as a whole, an average two women a week are killed by a male partner or former partner—this constitutes about one-third of all female homicide victims.

Family Violence in Scotland: Facts and Figures

- REPORTED cases of domestic violence have increased markedly in Scotland, with recent figures showing a rise of almost 14 per cent in four years.

- In 2007–8, police recorded 49,655 incidents of domestic abuse, compared with 43,632 in 2004–5.

- Those most at risk of abuse are women aged 31 to 35, and it is estimated that one in five women in Scotland experiences domestic abuse at some stage.

- On average, Central Scotland Police receive 300 calls of domestic violence incidents every month. But campaigners say this is only the tip of the iceberg and many victims suffer in silence for many years.

- Research shows the average victim will have been subject to 35 incidents before they seek help. Charities are calling for more resources to tackle the issue so the early signs of abuse can be picked up at hospitals and clinics.

- In the UK [United Kingdom] as a whole, an average two women a week are killed by a male partner or former partner—this constitutes about one-third of all female homicide victims.

- Women's charities point out domestic abuse can affect any woman, regardless of her race, class, age, income or religion.

VIEWPOINT 7

In Japan, Spousal Abuse Remains Hidden

David McNeill and Chie Matsumoto

A 2001 law made spousal abuse a crime in Japan; however, many women still fear for their lives, according to the writers of this viewpoint. Domestic violence cases rose by 20 percent between 2007 and 2008. Nevertheless, the writers contend that spousal abuse remains largely hidden in Japanese culture because women are frightened and ashamed to report the crime. Some activists believe that police and judges often blame the victim for the abuse. David McNeill writes for the London Independent *and Chie Matsumoto is a Japanese journalist who often writes for the* Japan Times.

As you read, consider the following questions:

1. How has the 2001 domestic violence law been revised, according to the viewpoint?
2. What cosmetics retailing giant sponsored a public demonstration and march against domestic violence?
3. To what does Emi Yoshida say she owes her escape from her abusive husband?

David McNeill and Chie Matsumoto, "Speaking Out About Domestic Violence," *The Japan Times*, November 7, 2009. Copyright ©2009 *The Japan Times*. All rights reserved. Reproduced by permission.

Family Violence and Intimate Partner Abuse

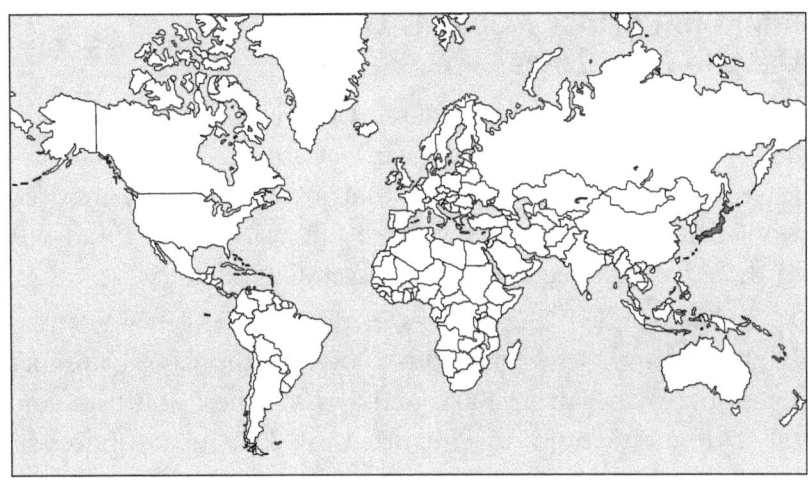

Just a year into her marriage, Emi Yoshida realized she might not survive it. Her violent, drug-addict husband had tried to strangle her, then beat her unconscious outside their Tokyo home. When she came to, he was threatening her with a knife.

Police offered no protection for her or her children. Instead of whisking her away to a battered wives' center, they tried to talk her into staying with her violent spouse, saying he "didn't mean" to inflict harm. "They said 'It's best the two of you talk it over,'" she recalled.

"If you beat up someone on the street, the police arrest you. But you're supposed to 'talk it over' when your partner is trying to kill you."

Now safe and happily in another relationship, the 29-year-old mother of three wants such violence treated as a crime like any other.

Legally, her demand has already been met: the 2001 Domestic Violence Law finally criminalized spousal abuse. The law has since been revised to include psychological abuse and threats, and allow for family restraining orders against abusive partners.

Intimate Partner Abuse Is Growing Despite New Laws

But despite—or perhaps because of this legislation—the number of victims grows year by year. A Cabinet Office survey released this year [2009] found that a quarter of all married women in Japan have experienced physical violence, and one in three has suffered verbal and psychological abuse.

Police handled 25,210 cases of domestic violence last year [2008], up by 20 percent from 2007 and the largest number since surveys began in 2002. Activists say those statistics, and the 77 domestic homicides reported in 2008, are an underestimate.

"The issue is hidden because many women are too frightened or ashamed to speak out," explained Fumi Suzuki, a lawyer and director of the Chiba-based Allies Law Office, which gives legal advice to battered wives. "Partly because of that, spousal abuse has a very low profile in Japan."

A [Japanese] survey ... found that a quarter of all married women in Japan have experienced physical violence, and one in three has suffered verbal and psychological abuse.

Suzuki was one of about 200 people who marched through Tokyo's Aoyama-Omotesando district last weekend [October 2009] in what was billed as Japan's first public demonstration by domestic violence victims.

Because many of the women (and a sprinkling of men) still live in fear of violent spouses, the route was kept secret and most of the marchers—and their children—wore Halloween masks.

In a sign of growing openness, however, the march was supported by cosmetics retailing giant The Body Shop. Social Democratic Party President Mizuho Fukushima, minister for gender equality in the new Democratic Party of Japan-led government, sent a letter of encouragement.

Some Tokyo shoppers along the route applauded the marchers, who held signs saying: "We are not to blame."

A Dissenting Opinion

All of which is a disaster for women, and men, according to Masako Nomaki.

"The (2001) law is infused with Communist ideology and is rooted in hatred of the family," said Nomaki, a teacher and conservative campaigner who wants the DV [domestic violence] legislation repealed. "Men and women can work out their problems if the government stays out of family life."

Nomaki accuses Fukushima and other supporters of the law of "brainwashing" women and trying to "destroy" society. "They render all the guilt on the male side, but male-female relationships cannot be reduced to laws and punishment."

"So-called victims of domestic violence provide courts with evidence that is faked, distorted and exaggerated,"

Outspoken conservative responses like that are rare.

Blaming the Victim

But the underlying assumption—that family is the bedrock of a stable society and should be immune to legal intervention—is not. Law or no, the police and courts still make life difficult for women looking for legal protection, argued lawyer Mami Nakano, who also represents domestic violence survivors.

She said police and judges sometimes blame the victims for provoking their husbands and are still wary of being proactive against violent partners in family disputes.

"I recently had to argue with a family-court judge about whether to leave a partition in place between my terrified client and the defendant."

Domestic Violence in Japan

Domestic violence (DV) is increasingly emerging from obscurity to be a serious issue in Japan. There is growing recognition that a number of Japanese women are victims of DV. According to a survey on DV conducted among 4500 people in 1998 by the Prime Minister's Office, one-third had experienced DV and 5 percent of the women who suffered from DV felt in danger of death....

DV is not a new problem: It has been around, concealed or condoned, for a long time, but it has only recently become a topic for discussion. The current attention on DV cases might reveal the incompatibility between changing lifestyles and attitudes of women and men's continuing belief in their essential superiority in a still male-dominated Japanese society.

Tokie Takahashi, "Domestic Violence in Japan,"
Tokyo Progressive, September 17, 2006.
http://tokyoprogressive.org.uk.

Fear, and the dearth of open public debate in Japan, keeps women silent. Even during last week's demonstration, many wore hunted expressions beneath the candy-colored masks.

One abuse survivor, who spoke on condition of anonymity, said she grew more anxious for her children as the march worked its way down Omotesando because spectators were taking photographs.

"I'm afraid that my ex-husband might get hold of some of these pictures somewhere and will learn about my children's whereabouts."

Suzuki acknowledges the sea change in legal protection for battered wives since the 1990s, when the issue finally began to percolate into public view.

"It's only quite recently—and not just in Japan—that governments began to recognize they must intervene in the family to stop violence."

But like many campaigners, she believes the state is still only halfheartedly dealing with domestic violence.

Financial insecurity and the loss of male confidence are traditional harbingers of interfamily violence.

"For example, women can now seek restraining orders, but once six months has lapsed they must go to court again and reapply. It's an ordeal, and if there has been no violence during that period a judge is likely to rule against her.

"It took a lot of courage for women to come out in public like this and demonstrate, so in that sense today's event is really very significant."

In at least one area, victims' lawyers and conservative opponents like Nomaki agree: Japan's deepening economic woes will increase tensions within society, and the home. Financial insecurity and the loss of male confidence are traditional harbingers of interfamily violence.

One Woman's Story

Yoshida said she owes her escape, along with her three children, to social workers and doctors who told her it was not her fault her husband was abusive. "They told me the children would be much better off without a father like that," she recalled.

Her husband was found dead in his apartment less than a year after their divorce became official. Yoshida was so traumatized from her beatings that for more than a month after his death, she was convinced he was playing a trick on her and was coming back. Even now, two years later, she says he still haunts her nightmares.

Now studying to become a nurse, her work and children, including a newborn, have helped her back on her feet.

"When I ran away, I made a commitment to cut the shackles that tied me to my husband and my children to the cycle of violence. Now I feel so free," she said while stroking her youngest daughter's hair. "I don't have to look around when I walk outside to see if he is chasing me."

VIEWPOINT 8

In the United States, Lesbian, Gay, Bisexual, and Transgender (LGBT) People Experience Intimate Partner Abuse

National Coalition of Anti-Violence Programs et al.

A 2007 report revealed that intimate partners within the lesbian, gay, bisexual, and transgender (LGBT) community sometimes are the perpetrators or victims of abuse. National Coalition of Anti-Violence Programs and colleagues summarize the tactics including verbal abuse, manipulation, assault, and stalking used by batterers against their intimate partners. In addition, the abuser sometimes resorts to making slurs against the sexual orientation of his or her partner, according to the authors. Members of the LGBT community often do not have access to protection or support afforded to other victims of family violence. NCAVP works to prevent, respond to, and end all forms of violence against and within lesbian, gay, bisexual, transgender, queer and HIV-affected (LGBTQH) communities. NCAVP is a national coalition of local member programs, affiliate organizations and individuals who create systemic and social change.

National Coalition of Anti-Violence Programs et. al., "Defining Intimate Partner Violence" and "The Impact of Homophobia & Transphobia," *Lesbian, Gay, Bisexual and Transgender Domestic Violence in the United States in 2007*, National Coalition of Anti-Violence Programs, 2008, pp. 5–7. www.ncavp.org. Copyright © 2008 by the National Coalition of Anti-Violence Programs. All rights reserved. Reproduced by permission.

Family Violence

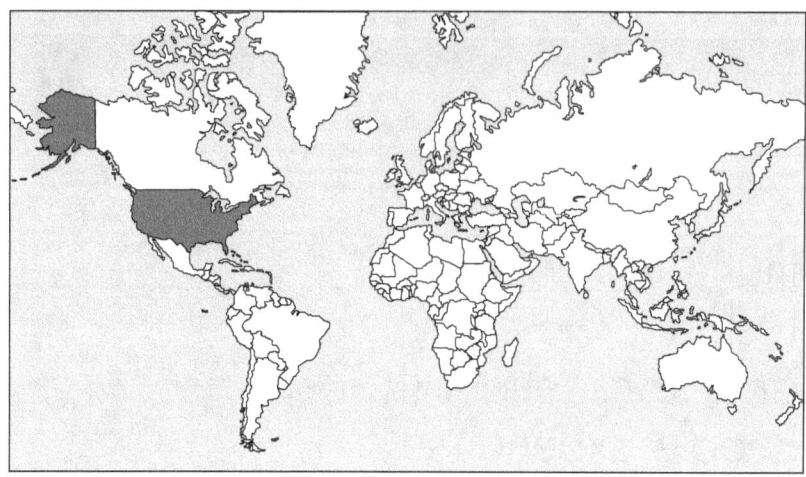

As you read, consider the following questions:
1. How is intimate partner violence defined by this viewpoint?
2. What might an abusive intimate partner limit or prohibit his or her partner from doing?
3. Attitudes rooted in multiple forms of oppression are pervasive in what institutions and facilities, according to the viewpoint?

NCAVP [National Coalition of Anti-Violence Programs] member programs encounter a range of types of intimate relationships presented by the survivors and batterers with whom we work. Patterns of power and control can emerge very quickly or they can develop slowly over time. An individual can experience ongoing violence from an individual with whom they had one sexual encounter or one date. Some of the people we work with would say they are in love with their partners and others would not. Some are married, some are exes, some are domestic partners, some live together, some are dating. Some would call their relationship long-term and others would not. There is a tremendous diversity in the identification of romantic relationships within LGBT [lesbian, gay, bisexual and transgender] communities. For this reason, we utilize "IPV [Intimate Partner Violence]" as a term that recognizes that diversity—that there is not one correct way to be in a relationship and that IPV is not endemic to any particular type of relationship. . . .

We define Intimate Partner Violence and Domestic Violence synonymously as "a pattern of behavior where one partner coerces, dominates, and isolates the other to maintain power and control over their partner."

Batterers often use racism, homophobia, transphobia, classism, ableism, immigration, and HIV status . . . to inflict harm.

Sources of Support

Survivors within almost any community often benefit from safety planning: assistance in noticing and in negotiating manipulative tactics and harm inflicted upon them by batterers. The types of harm they experience as well as the types of assistance that might be helpful, however, are very much impacted by their perceived or actual identities. Batterers often use racism, homophobia, transphobia, classism, ableism, immigration, and HIV status, even the batterers' own vulnerabilities, to inflict harm. When such tactics are used this compounds the effects of the violence and need for help. Support frequently comes from victim service providers in the form of shelter, safety planning, help with orders of protection and court accompaniment. The aim for most providers is to make available the best possible services to victims and survivors in order to help them develop the safest possible options given the particular circumstances of the abuse and the relationship.

Unfortunately, survivors from marginalized communities do not always receive services on par with those offered to mainstream survivors. As various cultures gain societal power and respect, they challenge inequities in myriad aspects of life, including IPV services.

Tactics of Abuse

Tools that may be used by the batterer to gain and maintain control are often highly individualized to the situation, relationship and people involved. It is important in any given situation of IPV to investigate the way the survivor defines the abuse and understand the ways that behaviors which we may not traditionally see as typically abusive can be utilized as such in a context where IPV already exists. However, there are several tactics that are commonly used by batterers against their victims. These behaviors may include:

- Verbal abuse, such as name-calling
- Emotional manipulation
- Isolation, including limiting or prohibiting a partner's contact with family or friends
- Stealing, limiting access to or destroying a partner's property
- Withholding or otherwise controlling or restricting access to finances
- Depriving partner of shelter, food, clothing, sleep, medication or any other life-sustaining mechanism
- Limiting or prohibiting a partner from obtaining or keeping employment, housing or any other station, benefit or service
- Harming or attempting to harm a partner physically
- Harming or threatening to harm a partner's family, friends, children and/or pets

Family Violence and Intimate Partner Abuse

- Sexually assaulting or raping a partner

- Using intentional exposure to sexually transmitted and other diseases

- Threatening suicide or harm to self, if a partner tries to end a relationship or does not comply with an abuser's demands

- Stalking or harassing a partner

- Using facets of abuser or survivor's identity including race, gender, class, sexual orientation, national origin, physical ability, religion, level of education, occupation, or legal immigration status, etc., to demean, insult, endanger, isolate, or otherwise oppress

Tactics Used Against LGBT Intimate Partners

All of the above tactics may be used by a batterer. There are additional concerns for LGBT survivors, many of which are specific to the survivor's queer identity or which exploit the survivor's gender identity or sexual orientation and the oppression they experience. Some of these tactics include:

- "Outing" or threatening to out a partner's sexual orientation or gender identity to family, employer, police, religious institution, community, or in child custody disputes

- Reinforcing fears that no one will help a partner because they are lesbian, gay, bisexual or transgender, or that for this reason, the partner "deserves" the abuse

- Alternatively, justifying abuse with the notion that a partner is not "really" lesbian, gay, bisexual or transgender; i.e., s/he may once have had or may still have

> ## The Scope of LGBT Intimate Partner Violence
>
> The number of studies designed to measure domestic violence in the LGBT [lesbian, gay, bisexual and transgender] community pale in comparison to their heterosexual counterparts. However, studies indicate the prevalence to be equal between the LGBT community and the heterosexual community. Results from the National Violence Against Women Survey indicated that gay males are more at risk than gay females. Approximately 23% of gay males studied reported to having been raped, physically assaulted, and/or stalked by another gay male. Slightly more than 11% of gay females also reported the same circumstances. With a victimization rate of approximately 10 to 25 percent, the statistics for either being abused or knowing someone who has been abused is alarming.
>
>
> Amy Menna,
> "Domestic Violence and the Gay Community:
> A Right to Peace and Safety," *Gift from Within*,
> December 28, 2010. www.giftfromwithin.org.
>

relationships with other people, or express a gender identity, inconsistent with the abuser's definitions of these terms

- Telling the partner that abusive behavior is a normal part of LGBT relationships, or that it cannot be domestic violence because it is occurring between LGBT individuals

- Using the reality of small LGBT communities to spread rumors and isolate the victim from social support

Multiple Forms of Oppression

It is important to note that all barriers present in both prevention and intervention of LGBT IPV and sexual assault are rooted in multiple forms of oppression. These attitudes, though often unspoken, are still pervasive in our police departments, court systems, medical centers, shelters, and organizations: The black butch lesbian in shelter who is watched more closely by staff; the low-income gay man who stays at all-night diners and couch hops with friends because he cannot access IPV shelter or homeless shelter; the transwoman immigrant with an expired visa who is arrested and placed in a men's jail cell along with her abusive boyfriend and then put in deportation proceedings; the Latino transman who is denied an order of protection in court because the judge refuses to acknowledge that his girlfriend is a real threat to his safety. Policy and legislative change alone will not eliminate these barriers for our communities.

Publicly exposing the effects of heterosexism, homophobia, and transphobia within IPV and within our institutions helps combat the stigma inflicted upon LGBT people by breaking the conspiracy of silence that society demands of us. As LGBT people work to lift the stigma that keeps many of us shamed or silenced about our experiences of abuse, or wary of sharing our identity, we begin to move closer to a day when LGBT survivors are adequately and fairly provided services, including orders of protection, real safety planning, and shelter. And closer to a day when no single person experiences violence from those they love.

Periodical and Internet Sources Bibliography

The following articles have been selected to supplement the diverse views presented in this chapter.

Lollie Barr	"Words Can Bring You Down," *Sunday Telegraph* (Australia), April 4, 2010. www.dailytelegraph.com.au.
Janelle Conaway	"Domestic Violence and Justice in Guatemala," *Américas*, vol. 62, no. 5, September–October 2010, pp. 46–47.
Katalin Fábián	"Mores and Gains: The EU's Influence on Domestic Violence Policies Among Its New Postcommunist Member States," *Women's Studies International Forum*, vol. 33, no. 1, January–February 2010, pp. 54–67.
Mariama Kandeh	"African Women in UK Silently Suffer Domestic Violence," allAfrica.com, December 15, 2010. http://allafrica.com.
W.W.S. Mak, E.S.K. Chong, and M.M.F. Kwong	"Prevalence of Same-Sex Intimate Partner Violence in Hong Kong," *Public Health*, vol. 124, no. 3, March 2010, pp. 149–52.
Hannatu Musawa	"What's Love Got to Do With It?," *Leadership* (Nigeria), November 24, 2010. www.leadership.ng.
Susan B. Sorenson and Kristie A. Thomas	"Views of Intimate Partner Violence in Same- and Opposite-Sex Relationships," *Journal of Marriage and Family*, vol. 71, no. 2, May 2009, pp. 337–52.
Flor Wang	"Taiwan Sees Rise in Domestic Violence," *China Post*, June 7, 2009. www.chinapost.com.tw.
World Health Organization	*Preventing Intimate Partner and Sexual Violence Against Women: Taking Action and Generating Evidence*, 2010. www.who.int.

CHAPTER 2

Dowry Violence, Bride Burning, and Honor Killings

VIEWPOINT 1

In Pakistan, Dowry Disputes Lead to Violence

Rakhshinda Parveen

According to Rakhshinda Parveen, dowry is a wedding gift paid by a bride's family to a groom's family. In Pakistan, dowry has become the motivation for violence against brides. "Stove deaths" happen when a stove explodes and burns the bride to death; Parveen argues that most stove deaths result when a member of the husband's family sets the woman on fire or pushes her into the stove. With the death of the bride, the groom is free to remarry and collect an additional dowry. Parveen is the executive vice president of the Society for the Advancement of Community, Health, Education, and Training (SACHET).

As you read, consider the following questions:

1. What is *jahez*?
2. On average, in 1997, how many women were burnt weekly, according to the Lahore press?
3. What legislation did the government of Nawaz Sharif introduce in the mid-1990s?

My parents were born in India, I was conceived at Dhaka of East Pakistan and delivered at Karachi, Pakistan. This implies that I literally descend from the patriarchal belt of

Rakhshinda Parveen, "Dowry: A Socio-Cultural Perspective," Society for the Advancement of Community, Health, Education and Training," 2011. Copyright © 2011 by Dr. Rakhshinda Parveen. All rights reserved. Reproduced with permission.

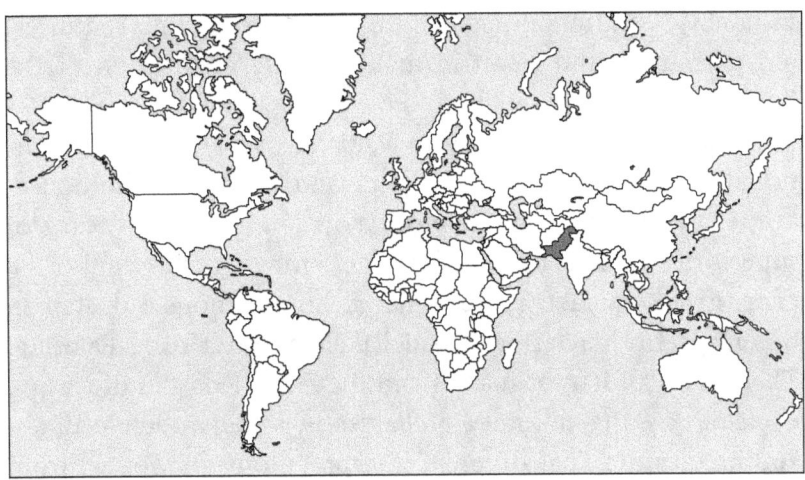

South Asia. The status gained by being born and brought up as a South Asian woman taught me about all the losses ordained by this position long before I learnt through international exposure, experience and education that this was the result of gender difference and gender discrimination. I am a woman, a medical doctor, a public health specialist, a teacher for Health Communication, a documentary filmmaker and a gender activist. All these are benign and powerless positions in a typical South Asian context. Therefore, I am a qualified nonspecialist to express myself on this subject.

Pakistan and Gender Violence

Violence against women is a global issue. Women have always been oppressed and abused intellectually, emotionally, physically and spiritually....

It would be too naïve to reject any violent practices in our homeland. Gender-based violence is one of the burning agenda items for social activists as it relates to condition, situation and position of men and women constituting the society.

The land of the pure [Pakistan] is characterized by regrettably low scores of development indicators, constant political instability, cultural heritage and traditions reflecting centuries-old patriarchy and selective male-friendly application of the dominant religion—Islam. For being part of the male-dominated belt, the family in Pakistan is patriarchal. Traditionally, father is the breadwinner and mother is the housekeeper. The disreputable mother-in-law is an advocate of superiority of her son in marriage. However, this cannot be generalized. In fact, there is not a homogenous Pakistan in this respect. There is an urban Pakistan and a rural Pakistan. There is a Pakistan of masses and there is a Pakistan of classes. Considering the diversity of Pakistani society, female plight and predicament has different interpretations for women from different strata. They do suffer similarly in different ways. Institutional and individual violence are not unknown phenomena for all Pakistani women.

Like all others, Pakistani society is governed by cultural institutions, beliefs, norms and practices. The contemporary culture, in spite of undergoing transition, mirrors images of centuries-old civilizations and indigenous cultures. One such cultural heritage which has been adopted as a cultural institution is dowry or *jahez*. This practice makes a girl-child less welcome than a male child. Even today, a girl is perceived to be a burden and a boy to be a blessing. No wonder there are 79 million missing women only in South Asia and Pakistan is one of those very few countries where male to female ratio is reverse[d].

> *Dowry is a multifaceted deep-rooted gender issue with social, economic and health consequences.*

A Definition of Dowry

What is dowry? Encyclopedias, thesauruses and dictionaries have explained it beautifully and simplistically. To me it is a form of culturally sanctioned and socially acceptable violence not only against women but men too. Despite relatively uninformed and unprepared acceptance of globalization as a way of life, it appears rather strange that the institution of marriage is still intact in Pakistan. Marriage is an important event in the life of a Pakistani woman. Getting married early is being lucky.

Obligatory *jahez* takes a heavy toll on the family of *dulhan*—the bride. Dowry is a multifaceted deep-rooted gender issue with social, economic and health consequences. In spite of a consensus on disliking the practice, only a few have the courage to disown it. According to renowned Indian writer Shri Sharma the "evolution" of dowry is originally from a gift creating expectation leading to demands and greed. A large dowry can be an important attribute of status to both men and women. Dowry, which is popularly considered as a Hindu custom, has visibly migrated, escalated and is embraced in all the areas of the present-day Pakistan. It has become an active tradition, norm and religious practice for those who believe that there is an absence of such custom and tradition in their faith. The implication of this convenient forgetfulness is inattentiveness to dowry-related violence.

There are certain other factors that ensure the continuity of the practice of dowry such as:

- It is considered an incentive to lure a more suitable match

- It is submission to the demand of a perceived suitable match

- It is used as an excuse for denial of inheritance to women (the expenses on dowry and wedding are unilaterally decided by the men folk of the family as transfer of inheritance by other means)

- It is considered a good support mechanism to help the new couple so that they have a convenient start in practical life

- It has become a socially forced fait accompli that is followed and executed 'with a smile' notwithstanding, how painful it could be to the family

In spite of very high frequency of domestic violence and frequent cases of stove deaths, dowry-related violence is neither perceived nor recognized as an accepted form of violence nor documented in social science literature.

Family Violence in Pakistan

Estimates of the percentage of women who experience domestic violence in Pakistan range from 70–90%. According to the Human Rights Commission of Pakistan (HRCP), the extreme form it took included driving a woman to suicide or engineering an accident through infamous "stove burning" usually when the husband, often in collaboration with his side of the family, felt (or made to believe) that the dowry or other gifts he had expected from his in-laws were not forthcoming or/and he wanted to marry again or he expected an inheritance from the death of his wife. During 1997, the Lahore press reported an average of more than four local cases of women being burnt weekly, three of the four fatally. Police follow-up to these cases was negligible, with only six suspects taken into custody out of 215 cases reported in Lahore newspapers during the year. In 1997, there was not a single conviction in a "stove death" case in the country.

HRCP reported only one case of dowry-related violence in 2001. In that case the victim was burnt to death by her in-laws for not bringing sufficient dowry. A research study conducted by SACHET [Society for the Advancement of Community, Health, Education and Training] on gender-based violence as reported in the print media also confirmed this statistic. Does this mean that in reality also, only one woman fell victim to dowry death? I sent one of our research officers to find some clues. Here is her back-to-office report.

Dowry Violence, Bride Burning, and Honor Killings

"I met Ms. Naheeda Mahboob Illahi, advocate Supreme court on 9th Jan 2002. According to her, every day a large number of cases of dowry-related violence are received but are mostly registered as domestic disputes. The details of only three cases of dowry-related violence were provided—2 cases in the year 2000 and one in 1997. In all these cases the victims were tortured mentally and physically by their husbands and in-laws, for not bringing sufficient dowry with them."

It remains a mystery for the social science researchers why stoves burst in *susrals* [the husband's family home] only and why the victim is always a *bahu* [daughter-in-law]? Ironically, in spite of very high frequency of domestic violence and frequent cases of stove deaths, dowry-related violence is neither perceived nor recognized as an accepted form of violence nor documented in social science literature. Therefore, unfortunately it is not a popular theme or priority agenda item for organizations working on women issues. There could be three possible reasons for this convenient forgetfulness. One is the spiral of silence and *sharam* [shame], which implies that woman-related issues must not be taken out of the premises of home for the sake of honor. Second is the ironical fact that attention to the role of dowry in our marriage system has not gained deserved attention of international donors. Therefore, the hype stirred by comparable social problems like child labor or environment overshadowed a traditional area like dowry and related issues. Thirdly, the ministry of women development in Pakistan has yet to acknowledge dowry and dowry violence as gender issues.

Dowry Has Not Yet Been the Subject of Intervention

Pakistan is a signatory to the International Conference on Population and Development (ICPD), Beijing [Declaration and Platform for Action] and [United Nations (UN)] Convention on the Elimination of All Forms of Discrimination

> ## Dowry Leads to Gender Violence
>
> In Pakistan, there are cultural barriers, beliefs and practices that weaken women's self-sufficiency and [act] as fuel to gender-based violence. Marriage practices lead towards paralyzing women even further.... Over the past few years dowry has become the integral part of marriage.... This increasing demand for dowry prevails in all classes; it is in the form of prerequisites and post-payment to marriages and a woman's security. Inability to match the demands results into harassment, physical violence and emotional abuse. In extreme cases murder or "stove burns" and suicides can provide husbands an opportunity to pursue another marriage and consequently more dowry.
>
> Hamza Ameer,
> "Increasing Ignorance of Women in Pakistani Society,"
> Asia Despatch, *January 2011. www.asiadespatch.com.*

Against Women (CEDAW). In terms of implementation, the ideals of all such treaties are yet to be realized to cast an impact. Empowerment, access to equal rights and emancipation are yet only distant dreams for a vast majority of women.

However, there are a number of efforts now under way in Pakistan to promote the empowerment of women, such as attempts to refine the National Plan of Action, develop microcredit plans and enhance Khushhali (prosperity) Bank, implement UN conventions and develop positive and productive partnerships with civil society, the CSOs [civil society organizations] and the private sector.

Personally, I am convinced that there is growing attention being given by the government to gender issues including violence, and there is some movement in this direction. But there is no obvious, focused and concentrated effort geared to the

Dowry Violence, Bride Burning, and Honor Killings

understanding of a complex and common issue like dowry. This is valid for all service delivery, advocacy, research and communication interventions.

Efforts made by mushrooming CSO sector in connection with dowry can be summed up as disappointing.

There had been localized and limited efforts by small-scale welfare societies in the 1960s and 1970s aiming at awareness raising and motivation campaigns to convince people at the mohalla level to resist the mindless following of dowry demands. However, with the advent of international donors in the 1980s, the CSOs in Pakistan have either [undertaken] campaigns against other more visibly anti-women oppressive mechanisms like hudood ordinance [Islamic law enforcing punishment of women] or political marginalization under the [Pakistani President Muhammad] Zia[-ul-Haq] regime. Later too, the CSOs have taken up issues of expressed violence thus being symptomatic and not delving into the deep-rooted causes of violence against women, dowry being one primary cause.

Taking notice of the visible exclusion of dowry as a gender issue from the agenda and aims of development CSOs and self-acclaimed gender experts, I initiated a fight against dowry [FAD] through the platform of SACHET, which I co-founded nearly five years back. FAD has been shaped into a project in Jan '02. The main objective of this project, rather a movement, is to eradicate (the institution and practice of) dowry in Pakistan. The key strategies to achieve this aim are research and communication. The activity spectrum ranges from surveys, signature campaigns, e-petitions, youth-parent consultations, legal advice, amendments in the existing law, lobbying, TV programs to anything possible under the sun.

The Government of Mr. Nawaz Sharif [former prime minister of Pakistan] in the mid-1990s had introduced an ordinance banning grand wedding receptions (an implicit upshot of dowry). However, it was enforced for a short time only, but is now losing its spirit. Right now, [Law & Justice Commission] has drafted a new law in connection with wedding expenses and dowry. The consultation on the draft version is in progress.

Challenges, Not Conclusions

Such write-ups usually conclude by drawing conclusions and making suggestions. I am concluding by identifying some of the challenges connected with the gruesome practice of dowry and the accompanying violence.

- How dowry could be made a high priority agenda to create a critical mass to combat this institutional violence?

- Are we ready to adopt this extremely critical gender issue as a passion?

- Is our mass media mature enough to advocate and sensitize all stakeholders?

- Do we have any political commitment in this regard and how far are our governments ready to go in this respect?

VIEWPOINT 2

In India, Bride Burning Is a Significant Problem

Nehaluddin Ahmad

According to Nehaluddin Ahmad, an increasing number of young Indian women are being burned alive, beaten to death, or pushed to commit suicide by their husbands and their husbands' families, who often perpetrate such violence as the result of disputes over dowries. A dowry is a monetary gift given by the bride's family to the groom. Ahmad argues that the dowry system reinforces the low social value of women and places hardship on the bride's family. Despite the violence caused by the dowry system, it is increasing its hold on Indian society. Ahmad is a university lecturer in Malaysia.

As you read, consider the following questions:

1. How many women in India commit suicide every four hours on average over dowry disputes?
2. What is the root cause of bride burning and other forms of domestic violence, according to Ahmad?
3. In what areas of India is the dowry system more rigid, according to Ahmad?

Dowry system as a social problem has acquired grave dimensions in recent years and all attempts for a legal solution have not produced the desired result. Over the past few

Nehaluddin Ahmad, "Introduction: Dowry Deaths (Bride Burning) in India and Abetment of Suicide: A Socio-Legal Appraisal," *Journal of East Asia and International Law*, October 2008, pp. 275–278. Copyright © 2008 by the Yijun Institute of International Law. All rights reserved. Reproduced by permission.

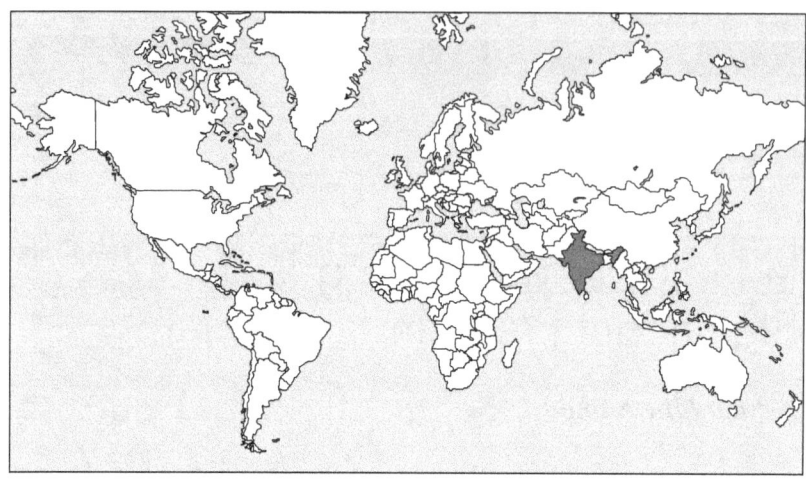

years, the cases of bride burning have registered a sharp increase throughout India, every day, almost every six hours, somewhere at some place in India, a young married woman is being burnt alive or beaten to death or being pushed to commit suicide. The gravity of the situation may also be judged from the fact that the National Commission for Women has recommended for the scrapping of the Dowry Prohibition Act. It only shows that the reality of the situation is beyond the legislative and enforcement activities. According to data compiled by the National Crime Records Bureau (NCRB) of India, a total of 2,276 female suicides due to dowry disputes were reported in 2006 that is six a day on an average, while the figure was 2,305 in 2005. In 2004, at least 2,385 such cases were registered across the country. On an average one Indian woman commits suicide every four hours over a dowry dispute, as per official data, despite a series of laws to empower them.

Dowry has been referred [to] and may [be] defined as "unilateral transfer of resources from the bride's family at marriage to the groom's family for inviting her to their home permanently and that dowry is, therefore, a compensatory payment to the family which agrees to shelter her hypothetically for the rest of her life."

Dowry Rules Society

The dowry custom continues to rule society. In majority of Indian families the boy has inheritance rights while the girl is given a hefty sum at the time of her marriage in lieu of the government-regulated equal rights for girls in parental property. The evil of the dowry system has spread its tentacles in almost all parts of the country and almost in every section of society. There are several reasons for the prevalence of the dowry system, but the main one is that it is a necessary precondition for marriage. "No dowry, no marriage," is a widespread fear. There has also been an emergence of a feudal mind-set with a materialistic attitude in a new globalized economy. The price tag for the groom is now bigger and bolder. The emergence of an affluent middle class, the torchbearer of social change in modern India, is the main factor for the perpetuation of the dowry system. It is difficult for families with daughters who are highly educated to arrange marriages because the girls are required to have even more educated husbands and there is shortage of eligible educated grooms. The daughter's parents are ready to pay a handsome amount as dowry and they run behind the eligible educated grooms.

> *There are several reasons for the prevalence of the dowry system, but the main one is that it is a necessary precondition for marriage.*

Most marriages are arranged by families, and a man who does not marry for love, he can marry for other considerations such as possessions. For this man and his family, a woman becomes the ticket to his shortcut to richness through the system of dowry. There are a number of things people desire to have in their own houses but cannot afford; they use the opportunity of a son's marriage to get them.

Family Violence

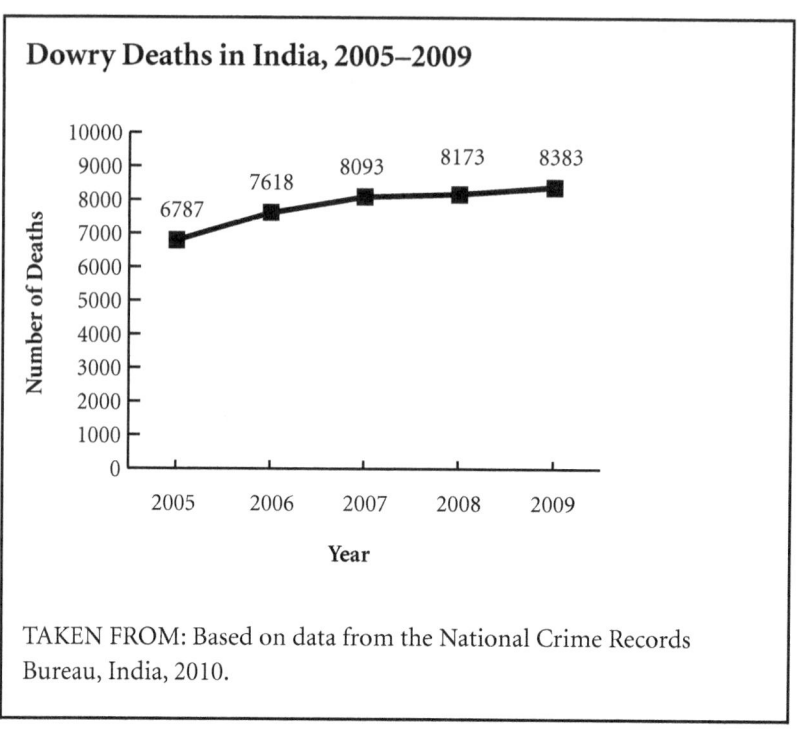

TAKEN FROM: Based on data from the National Crime Records Bureau, India, 2010.

On the other hand it is the duty of the father of the bride to find a suitable bridegroom for his daughter. The caste system; limited number of bread-earning and educated bridegrooms; lack of education and earning potential of brides; and greed of the bridegroom or his family to enrich by marriage have contributed the ancient system into a present practice.

Dowry and Bride Burning

The root cause of bride burning, as well as other forms of domestic violence against women, lies in their subordination and their frequent powerlessness within their husbands' family following marriage. Thus, cases of bride burning can and do occur without dowry being the causal factor, although dowry is possibly the single largest cause. Dowry commonly refers to the material gifts given to the bride by her family, usually at the time of the wedding. Scholars, such as M.N. Srinivas, make a distinction between the ancient custom of dowry as dakshina or dana (voluntary and often token gifts) and the contemporary practice of dowry. Nowadays dowry refers to material objects demanded (as opposed to voluntarily given) by the bridegroom's family, and often involves significant amounts of cash, property, household objects, and jewellery. In its current form, dowry is regarded, by those who demand it, as a reflection of the social status of the bridegroom's family. Thus, the more eligible the prospective bridegroom (eligibility being perceived as the social standing, the wealth, the educational and career-related achievements, and so forth, of himself and his family) the larger the dowry that his family has the right to demand and receive. Geraldine Forbes, and other scholars also point out that, in relatively recent times, growing consumerism and the increasing tendency to equate social status with material objects has made it attractive for prospective bridegrooms and their families to use the dowry as a means of enriching themselves at the time of marriage by demanding expensive presents from the parents of the prospective bride. The desire for continuing to benefit materially from the parents of the bride can take the form of pressuring the bride and her family for more dowry even after marriage.

Dissatisfaction over dowry may find expression through acts of hostility ranging from verbal abuse ... to bride burning.

Incidentally, the relatively low social value of girls in Indian society (manifest, for example, in the very recent custom, within some segments of Indian society, of aborting female fetuses) is connected to the financial pressures encountered by their families through the custom of dowry. There are few more motivations which could also motivate the dowry system such as:

- Aspiration to marry in the high and rich family.
- Pressure of the caste system.
- Social custom.
- Marriage system.
- False notion of social status.
- Vicious circle.

Dowry and Suicide

The pressure to provide a dowry is also felt by female children themselves. In Kanpur (Uttar Pradesh) three sisters were reported to have committed suicide in order to spare their parents the humiliation of not being able to provide a dowry, without which they could not get married. It is well known that the birth of a daughter is not a happy event. Giving birth to a daughter means additional burden of expenses of her marriage and endless expenses thereafter. The birth of a boy is an occasion for rejoicing. Women who give birth to sons get special favours from husbands and in-laws of some communities.

Dissatisfaction over dowry may find expression through acts of hostility ranging from verbal abuse to actual violence to bride burning. It is the most extreme violence against newly married women. This system is more rigid in the northern region consisting of Bihar, Uttar Pradesh, Rajasthan, Haryana, Delhi, Madhya Pradesh and states specially in the Hindi-speaking belt of India, but we cannot assume that non-Hindi-speaking provinces had no causality of dowry.

VIEWPOINT 3

In Bangladesh, the Custom of Dowry Leads to Abuse

Kaushalya Ruwanthika Ariyathilaka

In the following viewpoint, the author argues that marriage can be a deadly event for women in Bangladesh. Despite laws that ban the dowry system, it is still widely practiced. Often after marriage, men will demand a larger dowry than the one agreed upon and will beat their wives until their families comply. Dowry-related domestic violence blocks the economic development of the country, asserts the author, and more must be done to protect women. Kaushalya Ruwanthika Ariyathilaka is a staff writer for Dispatches International.

As you read, consider the following questions:

1. What two laws did the government of Bangladesh pass in the 1980s under pressure from human rights groups and the international community?
2. About how many girls in Bangladesh are already married between the ages of fifteen and seventeen?
3. What three efforts must be made to tackle dowry-related violence, according to Dr. Saira Rahman Khan?

"I am so scared. I am scared that my family will be broken. I don't want my children to live without a father or a mother. He tells me, 'Daughter of a beggar, go away. I don't

Kaushalya Ruwanthika Ariyathilaka, "A Wife's Darkest Hour: Dowry Violence in Bangladesh," *Dispatches International*, October 20, 2010. Copyright © 2010 by Dispatches International. All rights reserved. Reproduced by permission.

95

Family Violence

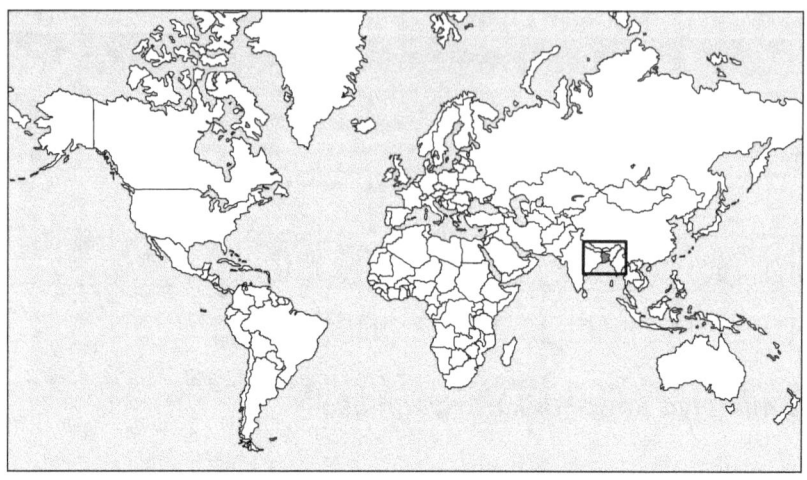

need you.' He also says that I am only good for beating." Shaheen, a young woman in Bangladesh who does not even know how old she is, reveals the dark side of her married life. She is married to Mohhamed Shohag, a carpenter by profession. Shaheen has spent most of her marriage suffering through abuse.

For the past eight years, Shaheen has been beaten by her husband for the same reason time and again: the demand for a dowry. According to Shaheen, her husband's family did not demand a dowry at her marriage. Yet, her husband changed his mind after the fact and asked her family to give a dowry. Shaheen's family was unable to meet his demand, and Shaheen ended up being punished for her family's inability to provide a dowry. Shaheen thinks living with a husband that physically and emotionally abuses her every day is her fate, and that she cannot do anything about it. Absolutely refusing the idea of complaining against her husband, Shaheen says, "I have never gone inside the police. I have to live with him, right? So how will I go to the police? I don't want to talk against my husband."

Shaheen is just another example of hundreds of thousands of young married women who are beaten nearly to death by their husbands every day. "We, women, are helpless. There is no one to help us. Who is there to help us, to stop our husbands beating us? No one likes to be beaten. It hurts a lot." With these words, she unveils the story of spousal abuse and other forms of violence against women in Bangladesh. This violence takes various forms such as battering, domestic and dowry-related violence, acid attacks, rape, fatwa (the Islamic law issued by an Imam, the leader of a mosque), sexual harassment in the workplace, and even human trafficking.

Marriage Is No Heaven for Brides

Even before marriage, women suffer in Bangladesh. Girls are fed last and least, and are often seen as a burden; this is typical in most South Asian countries. Parents see marriage as a safe way to get rid of their daughters. Unfortunately, girls find no heaven in their marital houses because some families demand a dowry from their daughters-in-law. While Bangladesh recognizes Islam as its official religion, dowry continuously contradicts both religion and the law. According to the Qu'ran [the sacred book of Islam] receiving dowry from the bride's family is *haram*, forbidden by the Islamic law; it is the husband's family that should provide *mohorana*, money for the bride's family.

Statistics show that 88% of the recently married Muslim wives in Dhaka, the capital of Bangladesh, did not receive their *mohorana*, but were forced to give a dowry. Even though girls and women are forced to wear the *burqa* [a long, loose garment that covers the face and body], as a means for following the guidelines of the Qu'ran, people easily forget about religion when it comes to taking or demanding a dowry. "It has become a practice to give dowry to the groom's family to show gratitude that he has agreed to marry the bride. But the truth is, it has become a kind of source of income for the groom and an easy way to get money without working for it," explains Dr. Saira Rahman Khan, an assistant professor at the

School of Law at the Bangladesh Rural Advancement Committee (BRAC) University and a founding member of Odhikar, a leading nongovernmental organization [NGO] working to raise awareness on human rights abuses in Bangladesh. According to Khan, "social pressure on the bride's family and fear" are the factors that keep nurturing the dowry system—despite the fact that it is legally banned.

Parents see marriage as a safe way to get rid of their daughters. Unfortunately, girls find no heaven in their marital houses.

No Decrease in Violence, Despite Laws

Under enormous pressure from human rights groups and the international community, the Bangladeshi government passed the Dowry Prohibition Act in 1980, which legally banned dowries and imposed sanctions, as well as the Cruelty to Women Ordinance in 1983. Yet, incidents of domestic violence due to dowry issues have not decreased. The government of Bangladesh imposed the Women and Children Repression Prevention Act in 2000 that enhanced the punishment up to death penalty for crimes against women and children, depending on the incident. As a result of this law, taking or demanding a dowry could result in imprisonment, a fine, or both.

"I do not see any decrease in the trend, despite the fact that there is a Dowry Prohibition Act in place and several large NGOs and government initiatives to stop violence against women," says Khan, explaining the factors that are conducive to the continuation of dowry-related violence in Bangladesh: "lack of implementation of laws, lack of political will of the government, the perception of domestic violence as a social matter, ingrained 'traditions,' and especially the overall corruption that directly and indirectly influences all of the above."

Md. Shah Alam, the second officer of the Khulshi Police Station in Chittagong, speaks gravely about the limitations the law itself encounters. "Police or the court can't stop people. We can't put each and every person in jail," he says, citing the experiences of his colleagues at the police station. "So we have to make sure that people know it is a bad thing, you know to beat their wife or to ask them to give money."

Shaheen Begum (a different woman than the Shaheen quoted at the beginning of this [viewpoint]) has been an outspoken critic of the status quo since her second husband's death. She says that even though she tries to increase consciousness among her neighbors, her attempts are often fruitless. "People ask to tell the police. But they don't do it, it brings more problems to those girls," she says. "They don't want to live without a husband, without a family. And then they are scared that their husband's family will kill them."

What has made the women in Bangladesh prisoners of their own reluctance? Hafeeza, Shaheen's sister-in-law who is also a victim of dowry-associated domestic violence, thinks she has an answer: the ability of Bangladeshi men to divorce their wives. "He will divorce me right now, he just has to say talaq," says Hafeeza. "He has money, so it will be not a problem for him. He says, 'Go to police if you want,' because the police can't do anything for me."

Tragically, while Mohhamed Shohag beats his wife—Hafeeza's sister—demanding a dowry, his sister is being beaten up by her own husband, for the same reason. "He said I was like dust in his eyes. He doesn't like me. He said, 'You are just spending my money, you came here even without a dowry; how shameless you are!' and other things like that." Hafeeza feels sympathy for her sister-in-law, yet she thinks her own situation is far worse. "He beats me too much. Her [Shaheen's] beatings are nothing compared to mine." . . .

> ## The Never-Ending Dowry
>
> Dowry has come to be one of the most critical sources of capital for all families. It is not only practiced as a one-off payment during marriage, but many families continue to use their newly married incoming wives as an ongoing source of capital, by sending them back to their natal home again and again to bring back more capital. If the wives' families cannot oblige, the wives are subjected to violence, or even divorce.
>
> Santi Rozario, "The Dark Side of Micro-Credit," Open Democracy, December 10, 2007. www.opendemocracy.net.

The Fate of Bangladeshi Girls

Unfortunately, despite all the negative ramifications and the legal and religious boundaries, dowry does prevail in Bangladesh. Dowries are frequent and common, although they are never spoken of publicly, "Here, people give dowries secretively. No one tells others that they are giving dowries. Money, jewelries, and other things they give secretively. . . . Because, in our religion, it's not good to give dowry. We, Biharis, shouldn't give dowries," says Shaheen. Even though keeping up with the dowry system is not appropriate according to the law and religion, it is a matter of status. Khan, the professor at BRAC University, explains, "It is a means of ensuring that the bride is not abused or mistreated in her husband's house."

But, does a dowry really make sure that the bride is well cared for? According to a study done in 2004, women who pay a dowry are very likely to face domestic violence, even in comparison to those who do not pay a dowry. Furthermore, those who pay small dowries are more likely to be subjected to domestic violence than those who pay larger ones. For some Bangladeshis, a dowry is the daughter's inheritance from the family, with all other property going to sons. A large dowry makes it possible to arrange a marriage with a boy from a family of higher social status. Yet, in reality, daughters often do not inherit anything other than physical and emotional abuse.

The majority of Bangladeshi girls' fates are decided when they are born. Bangladesh has one of the highest rates of child marriage in the world. More than two-thirds of adolescent girls get married. About two in every five girls who are between the ages of 15 and 17 are already married, regardless of the fact that 18 is the legal age for marriage. Girls are less likely to have secondary or tertiary education, usually because they were married at such a young age. If they are lucky enough to get higher education, their dowry increases.

More than half of the adolescent girls in Bangladesh become mothers when they are 19 years old, and half of these are malnourished. The national maternal mortality rate is one of the worst in Asia; every year about 11,000 women die giving birth, as most deliveries take place at home without a skilled professional. One in every seven maternal deaths is due to domestic violence. Moreover, Bangladesh continues to be one of the few countries where the life expectancy of women is lower than that of men.

According to a study done in 2004, women who pay a dowry are very likely to face domestic violence, even in comparison to those who do not pay a dowry.

Dowry-Related Abuse Is a Major Threat to Bangladesh

Government and nongovernmental institutions are considering dowry-related domestic violence as a major threat to the development of the country and are developing new programs to assist women in need. "We have a special victim support center in Dhaka for women. There is a branch in Chittagong, too. We also have a separate court for women and child cases, it's under the women and child act," says Alam, the police officer in Chittagong. Unfortunately, few women—terrified of their husbands—take advantage of these resources. Khan explains why: "Complaints to the police will do no good. When her complaint reaches her husband's ears, all hell might break loose. If a wife is thrown out of her house by her husband, and she has no income or education, she has no option but to stay with her father. This becomes not only a matter of financial strain but also sometimes a matter of shame for her father's family."

Shaheen and Hafeeza, like many women in Bangladesh, think complaining to the police against their husbands is not justifiable. Furthermore, it will make their husbands angrier, which could lead to more physical abuse. They have made up their minds to face both the threat and use of force for the sake of sustaining their marriages. A woman without a husband or a family is often shunned by society in Bangladesh, and both women are unwilling to face such ostracism. "Many times I thought I would leave him and go somewhere. But later I think how people will talk about me if I leave my husband," says Hafeeza, trying to defend her decision. "They will say I ran away with another man. They will say I went against God's will. I would be a fool to run away."

Even though Hafeeza and Shaheen refuse to seek legal advice, they do understand the injustice of their situation. Hafeeza says, "I never support him [her brother-in-law, Shaheen's husband]. He is doing this to his wife, that's why he can't stop what my husband is doing to me. He doesn't realize that my husband is doing the same thing as he is doing. He should stop this. He shouldn't do this." Hafeeza also says, "If someone is being punished for his wrong, then the others will be scared from doing the same." But when asked about who should be responsible for bringing justice, she is silent.

Why would dowry drive men to be violent against their wives? What gives a man the courage even to kill his wife, if the dowry demand is not met? How can he justify murder?

Aggression tends to increase when the men understand that they could be better off financially if the wife brings a dowry.

Poverty Is the Major Factor in Dowry Violence

The major factor that is responsible for dowry-related violence is poverty. "Poverty is one of the leading causes of domestic violence. The majority of battered women who come to us are from poor households," says Fauzia Karim, of the Bangladesh [National] Women Lawyers Association. Having no proper income to maintain a family makes husbands demand a dowry, meaning that his wife is another mouth to feed, a burden if she does not come with the money that would provide for her support.

Poverty, along with a retinue of other social problems, makes husbands, the traditional breadwinners of Bangladeshi families, more prone to being violent. They seek equality by beating their wives, who they see as not having to struggle for a living. Aggression tends to increase when the men understand that they could be better off financially if the wife brings a dowry. Thus, dowry-related violence cannot be eliminated unless poverty is reduced.

Khan ... gives her opinion on ending violence against women in Bangladesh. She calls for three efforts to tackle dowry-related violence: first, strong political will to bring about change; second, an end to the corruption and misuse of the police system; third, and perhaps most important, more affirmative action from organizations so that they actually stop the violence and not sustain it so as to sustain their own funding.

VIEWPOINT 4

In Iraq, Honor Killings Subjugate Women

Terri Judd

Terri Judd reports in the following viewpoint on teenage girls in Iraq who have been murdered by their fathers and other family members for "dishonoring" their families by doing such things as having unknown numbers on their cell phones, falling in love with the wrong boy, and wearing clothing that breaks Islamic dress codes. Government officials are reluctant to interfere when it comes to the issue of honor killings. Activists call for the international community to help protect Iraqi women from the violence. Judd is a journalist who writes for the Independent.

As you read, consider the following questions:

1. How many women a month are murdered in Basra for breaking Islamic dress codes, according to the viewpoint?
2. What Kurdish member of Parliament has been called on to outlaw honor killings?
3. How many women were beheaded in Mosul in 2006 in a terror campaign?

Terri Judd, "Barbaric 'Honour Killings' Become the Weapon to Subjugate Women in Iraq," *The Independent*, April 28, 2008. Copyright © 2008 by *The Independent*. All rights reserved. Reproduced with permission.

Family Violence

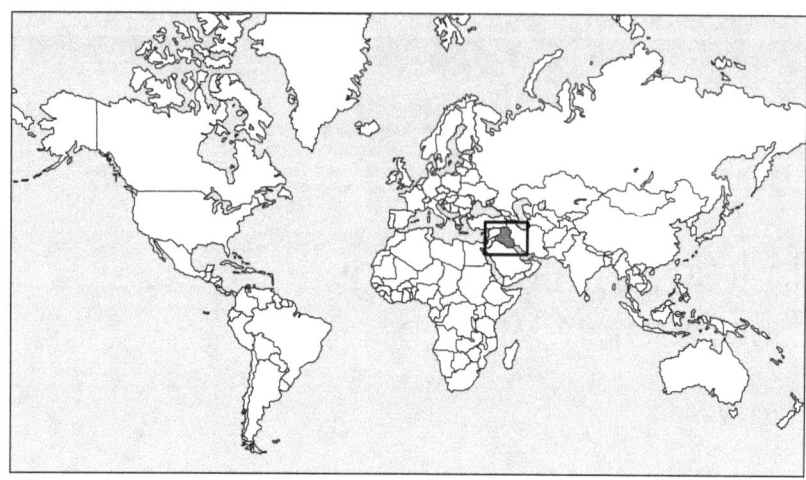

At first glance Shawbo Ali Rauf appears to be slumbering on the grass, her pale brown curls framing her face, her summer skirt spread about her. But the awkward position of her limbs and the splattered blood reveal the true horror of the scene.

Murdered by Her Family

The 19-year-old Iraqi was, according to her father, murdered by her own in-laws, who took her to a picnic area in Dokan and shot her seven times. Her crime was to have an unknown number on her mobile phone. Her "honour killing" is just one in a grotesque series emerging from Iraq, where activists speak of a "genocide" against women in the name of religion.

In the latest such case, it was reported yesterday [April 27, 2008] that a 17-year-old girl, Rand Abdel-Qader, was stabbed to death last month by her father for becoming infatuated with a British soldier serving in southern Iraq.

In Basra alone, police acknowledge that 15 women a month are murdered for breaching Islamic dress codes. Campaigners insist it is a conservative figure.

Violence against women is rampant, rising every day with the power of the militias. Beheadings, rapes, beatings, suicides through self-immolation [setting oneself on fire], genital mutilation, trafficking and child abuse masquerading as marriage of girls as young as nine are all on the increase.

Du'a Khalil Aswad, 17, from Nineveh, was executed by stoning in front of [a] mob of 2,000 men for falling in love with a boy outside her Yazidi tribe. Mobile phone images of her broken body transmitted on the Internet led to sectarian violence, international outrage and calls for reform. Her father, Khalil Aswad, speaking one year after her death in April last year, has revealed that none of those responsible had been prosecuted and his family remained "outcasts" in their own tribe.

"My daughter did nothing wrong," he said. "She fell in love with a Muslim and there is nothing wrong with that. I couldn't protect her because I got threats from my brother, the whole tribe. They insisted they were [going] to kill us all, not only Du'a, if she was not killed. She was mutilated, her body dumped like rubbish.

"I want those who committed this act to be punished but so far they have not, they are free. Honour killing is murder. This is a barbaric act."

Honour Killings on the Rise

Despite the outrage, recent calls by the Kurdish MP [member of Parliament] Narmin Osman to outlaw honour killings have been blocked by fundamentalists. "Honour killings are not actually a crime in the eyes of the government," said Houzan Mahmoud, who has had a fatwa [an Islamic ruling] on her head since raising a petition against the introduction of sharia law in Kurdistan. "If before there was one dictator persecuting people, now almost everyone is persecuting women.

"In the past five years it . . . has got [much] worse. It is difficult to describe how terrible it is, how badly we have been pushed back to the dark ages. Women are being beheaded for taking their veil off. Self-immolation is rising—women are left

> ## Murdered by Her Father
>
> It was [Rand Abdel-Qader's] first youthful infatuation and it would be her last. She died on 16 March [2008], after her father discovered she had been seen in public talking to Paul, considered to be the enemy, the invader and a Christian. Though her horrified mother, Leila Hussein, called Rand's two brothers, Hassan, 23, and Haydar, 21, to restrain Abdel-Qader as he choked her with his foot on her throat, they joined in. Her shrouded corpse was then tossed into a makeshift grave without ceremony as her uncles spat on it in disgust.
>
> Afif Sarhan and Caroline Davies,
"'My Daughter Deserved to Die for Falling in Love,'"
Observer, May 11, 2008.

with no choice. There is no government body or institution to provide any sort of support. Sharia law is being used to underpin government rule, denying women their most basic human rights."

In Sulaymaniyah [Kurdistan], a city of 1 million people, there were 407 reported offences, beheadings, beatings, deaths through "family problems", and threats of honour killings [in 2007].

In August last year [2007], the body of 11-year-old Sara Jaffar Nimat was found in Khanaqin, Kurdistan, after she had been stoned and burnt to death. Earlier this month, two brothers and a sister were kidnapped from their home near Kirkuk by gunmen in police uniforms. The brothers were beaten to death and the woman left in a critical condition after being informed that she must obey the rules of an "Islamic state". One week ago, a journalist, Begard Hussein, was murdered in her home in Arbil, northern Iraq. Her husband, Mohammed Mustafa, stabbed her because she was in love with another man, according to local reports.

The stoning death of Ms Aswad led to the establishment of an Internal Ministry unit in Kurdistan to combat violence against women. It reported that last year in Sulaymaniyah, a city of 1 million people, there were 407 reported offences, beheadings, beatings, deaths through "family problems", and threats of honour killings. Rape is not included as most women are too fearful to report it for fear of retribution. Nevertheless, police in Karbala recently revealed 25 reports of rape.

The new Iraqi constitution, according to Mrs Mahmoud, is a mass of confusing contradictions. While it states that men and women are equal under law it also decrees that sharia law—which considers one male witness worth two females—must be observed. The days when women could hold down key jobs or enjoy any freedom of movement are long gone. The fundamentalists have sent out too many chilling messages. In Mosul two years ago [2006], eight women were beheaded in a terror campaign.

"It was really, really horrifying," said Mrs Mahmoud. "Honour killings and murder are widespread. Thousands [of people] ... have become victims of murder, violence and rape—all backed by laws, tribal customs and religious rules. We urge the international community, the government to condemn this barbaric practice, and help the women of Iraq."

VIEWPOINT 5

The United States Should Differentiate Honor Killings from Domestic Violence

Phyllis Chesler

In the following viewpoint, Phyllis Chesler argues that honor killings are religiously based and not simply more examples of domestic violence. Honor killings are usually committed by Muslim fathers against their teenage daughters, although sometimes men murder their older daughters and wives. The reason given for the murders is that the women have dishonored the family; the men who commit the murders feel little remorse and claim it is their religious duty. Chesler is emerita professor of psychology and women's studies at City University of New York.

As you read, consider the following questions:

1. Why and by whom was Aqsa Parvez murdered in 2007?
2. How does Unni Wikan define honor killing?
3. How many Muslim immigrants and their descendents live in Europe, according to this viewpoint?

When a husband murders a wife or daughter in the United States and Canada, too often law enforcement chalks the matter up to domestic violence. Murder is murder; religion is irrelevant. Honor killings are, however, distinct

Phyllis Chesler, "Are Honor Killings Simply Domestic Violence?," *The Middle East Quarterly*, Spring 2009. Copyright © 2009 by *The Middle East Quarterly*. All rights reserved. Reproduced by permission.

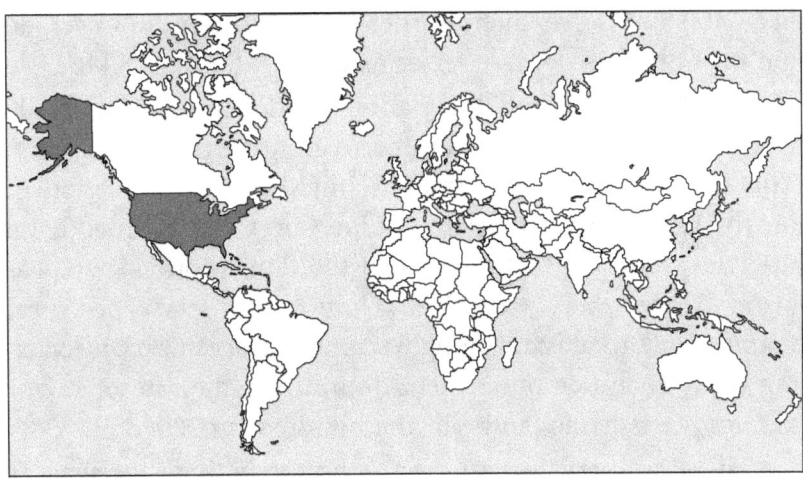

from wife battering and child abuse. Analysis of more than fifty reported honor killings shows they differ significantly from more common domestic violence. The frequent argument made by Muslim advocacy organizations that honor killings have nothing to do with Islam and that it is discriminatory to differentiate between honor killings and domestic violence is wrong.

Families Will Kill for Honor

Families that kill for honor will threaten girls and women if they refuse to cover their hair, their faces, or their bodies or act as their family's domestic servant; wear makeup or Western clothing; choose friends from another religion; date; seek to obtain an advanced education; refuse an arranged marriage; seek a divorce from a violent husband; marry against their parents' wishes; or behave in ways that are considered too independent, which might mean anything from driving a car to spending time or living away from home or family. Fundamentalists of many religions may expect their women to meet some but not all of these expectations. But when women refuse to do so, Jews, Christians, and Buddhists are far more likely to shun rather than murder them. Muslims, however, do kill for honor, as do, to a lesser extent, Hindus and Sikhs.

The United Nations Population Fund estimates that 5,000 women are killed each year for dishonoring their families. This may be an underestimate. Aamir Latif, a correspondent for the Islamist website Islam Online who writes frequently on the issue, reported that in 2007 in the Punjab province of Pakistan alone, there were 1,261 honor murders. The Aurat Foundation, a Pakistani nongovernmental organization focusing on women's empowerment, found that the rate of honor killings was on track to be in the hundreds in 2008.

There are very few studies of honor killing, however, as the motivation for such killings is cleansing alleged dishonor and the families do not wish to bring further attention to their shame, so do not cooperate with researchers. Often, they deny honor crimes completely and say the victim simply went missing or committed suicide. Nevertheless, honor crimes are increasingly visible in the media. Police, politicians, and feminist activists in Europe and in some Muslim countries are beginning to treat them as a serious social problem.

Willingness to address the problem of honor killing, however, does not extend to many Muslim advocacy groups in North America. The well-publicized denials of U.S.-based advocacy groups are ironic given the debate in the Middle East. While the religious establishment in Jordan, for example, says that honor killing is a relic of pre-Islamic Arab culture, Muslim Brotherhood groups in Jordan have publicly disagreed to argue the Islamic religious imperative to protect honor.

Honor Killings as an Islamic Imperative

Yotam Feldner, a researcher at the Middle East Media Research Institute, quotes a psychiatrist in Gaza who describes the honor killing culture as one in which a man who refrains from "washing shame with blood" is a "coward who is not worthy of living ... as less than a man." Therefore, it is no surprise that the Jordanian penal code is quite lenient towards honor killers. While honor killing may be a custom that originated in the pagan, pre-Islamic past, contemporary Islamist interpretations of religious law prevail. As Feldner puts it: "Some important Islamic scholars in Jordan have even gone further by declaring honor crimes an Islamic imperative that derives from the 'values of virility advocated by Islam.'"

Islamist advocacy organizations, however, argue that such killings have nothing to do with Islam or Muslims, that domestic violence cuts across all faiths, and that the phrase "honor killing" stigmatizes Muslims whose behavior is no different than that of non-Muslims. For example, in response to a well-publicized 2000 honor killing, SoundVision.com, an Islamic information and products site, published an article that argued,

> Four other women were killed in Chicago in the same month.... They were white, African-American, Hispanic, and Asian.... Islam is not responsible for [the Muslim woman's] death. Nor is Christianity responsible for the deaths of the other women.

In 2007, after Aqsa Parvez was murdered by her father in Toronto for not wearing *hijab* (a head covering), Sheila Musaji wrote in the *American Muslim*, "Although this certainly is a case of domestic violence ... 'honor' killings are not only a Muslim problem, and there is no 'honor' involved." Mohamed Elmasry, of the Canadian Islamic Congress, also dismissed the problem. "I don't want the public to think that this is an Islamic issue or an immigrant issue. It is a teenager issue," he said.

Indeed, denial is rife. In 2008, after Kandeela Sandal was murdered for honor by her father in Atlanta because she wanted a divorce, Ajay Nair, associate dean of multicultural affairs at Columbia University, told the media that "most South Asian communities in the United States" enjoy "wonderful" relationships within their families and said, "This isn't a rampant problem within South Asian communities. What is a problem, I think, is domestic violence, and that cuts across all communities." In October 2008, Mustafaa Carroll, executive director of the Dallas branch of the Council on American-Islamic Relations (CAIR), dismissed any Islamic connection to a prominent Dallas honor killing, labeled as such by the FBI [Federal Bureau of Investigation], arguing, "As far as we're concerned, until the motive is proven in a court of law, this is [just] a homicide." He continued, "We [Muslims] don't have the market on jealous husbands . . . or domestic violence. . . . This is not Islamic culture."

Case studies suggest otherwise.

Domestic Violence vs. Honor Killing

Domestic violence is a significant problem in the United States. Between 1989 and 2004, 21,124 women died at the hands of an intimate; 8,997 men died in domestic violence during the same time period. Because the U.S. Department of Justice does not catalogue the victim's or murderer's age, religion, ethnic background, or immigration status, it is not possible to know what proportion of these killings are honor related.

Unni Wikan, a social anthropologist and professor at the University of Oslo, defines honor killing as "a murder carried out as a commission from the extended family, to restore honor after the family has been dishonored. As a rule, the basic cause is a rumor that any female family member has behaved in an immoral way." While honor killings are just a minority of total domestic violence in the United States and Canada, they constitute a distinct phenomenon. A 2008 Massachusetts-based study found that "although immigrants make up an estimated 14 percent of the state's population, [they, nevertheless,] accounted for 26 percent of the 180 domestic violence deaths from 1997–2006."

Lenore Walker, author of *The Battered Woman Syndrome*, agreed that fundamentalist immigrants control and patrol their women very closely. "Given the strict rules, there are a lot of things to kill them for," she said. Walker confirmed the difference between the victim-perpetrator in honor killings and ordinary domestic violence:

> In ordinary domestic violence involving Westerners, it is rare for brothers to kill sisters or for male cousins to kill female cousins. And while child abuse occurs in which fathers may kill infants and children, it is very rare for Western fathers to kill teenage daughters.

Muslims who commit or assist in the commission of honor killings view these killings as heroic and even view the murder as the fulfillment of a religious obligation.

Other discrepancies exist. Walker observed that Western men are more apt to kill little boys than girls in their family. "Women with postpartum depression kill their babies, and men may kill babies by shaken baby syndrome," she explained. She did not "know of any batterers who are helped to commit the murders by their brothers or cousins or other family members. Occasionally, the man's relatives may be in the house when the murder goes down, but that is quite rare in my experience."

The press has reported a number of honor killings in the United States, Canada, and Europe. These cases show the killings to be primarily a Muslim-on-Muslim crime. The victims are largely teenage daughters or young women. Wives are victims but to a lesser extent. And, unlike most Western domestic violence, honor killings are carefully planned. The perpetrator's family may warn the victim repeatedly over a period of years that she will be killed if she dishonors her family by refusing to veil, rebuffing an arranged marriage, or becoming too Westernized. Most important, only honor killings involve multiple family members. Fathers, mothers, brothers, male cousins, uncles, and sometimes even grandfathers commit the murder,

Family Violence

Honor Killings Compared to Domestic Violence

Honor Killings	Domestic Violence
Committed mainly by Muslims against Muslim girls/young adult women.	Committed by men of all faiths, usually against adult women.
Committed mainly by fathers against their teenage *daughters* and daughters in their early twenties. Wives and older-age daughters may also be victims, but to a lesser extent.	Commited by an adult male spouse against an adult female spouse or intimate partner.
Carefully planned. Death threats are often used as a means of control.	The murder is often unplanned and spontaneous.
The planning and execution involve multiple family members and can include mothers, sisters, brothers, male cousins, uncles, grandfathers, etc. If the girl escapes, the extended family will continue to search for her to kill her.	The murder is carried out by one man with no family complicity.
The reason given for the honor killing is that the girl or young woman has "dishonored" the family.	The batterer-murderer does not claim any family concept of "honor." The reasons may range from a poorly cooked meal to suspected infidelity to the woman's trying to protect the children from his abuse or turning to the authorities for help.
At least half the time, the killings are carried out with barbaric ferocity. The female victim is often raped, burned alive, stoned or beaten to death, cut at the throat, decapitated, stabbed numerous times, suffocated slowly, etc.	While some men do beat a spouse to death, they often simply shoot or stab them.

[CONTINUED]

but mothers and sisters may lobby for the killing. Some mothers collaborate in the murder in a hands-on way and may assist in the getaway. In some cases, taxi drivers, neighbors, and mosque members prevent the targeted woman from fleeing,

Honor Killings Compared to Domestic Violence

Honor Killings (cont.)	**Domestic Violence** (cont.)
The extended family and community valorize the honor killing. They do not condemn the perpetrators in the name of Islam. Mainly, honor killings are seen as normative.	The batterer-murderer is seen as a criminal; no one defends him as a hero. Such men are often viewed as sociopaths, mentally ill, or evil.
The murderer(s) do not show remorse. Instead, they experience themselves as "victims," defending themselves from the girl's actions and trying to restore their lost family honor.	Sometimes, remorse or regret is exhibited.

TAKEN FROM: Phyllis Chesler, "Are Honor Killings Simply Domestic Violence?," *Middle East Quarterly*, Spring 2009.

report her whereabouts to her family, and subsequently conspire to thwart police investigations. Very old relatives or minors may be chosen to conduct the murder in order to limit jail time if caught.

Seldom is domestic violence celebrated, even by its perpetrators. In the West, wife batterers are ostracized. Here, there is an important difference in honor crimes. Muslims who commit or assist in the commission of honor killings view these killings as heroic and even view the murder as the fulfillment of a religious obligation. A Turkish study of prisoners found no social stigma attached to honor murderers. While advocacy organizations such as CAIR denounce any link between honor killings and Islam, many sheikhs still preach that disobedient women should be punished. Few sheikhs condemn honor killings as anti-Islamic. Honor killings are not stigmatized.

In both North America and Europe, family members conducted honor killings with excessive violence—repeatedly stabbing, raping, setting aflame, and bludgeoning—in more than half the cases. Only in serial-killing-type scenarios are Western women targeted with similar violence; in these cases, the perpetrators are seldom family members, and their victims are often strangers. Despite the obfuscation of Muslim advocacy groups, these case studies show that honor killings are quite distinct from domestic violence. Not all honor killings are perpetrated by Muslims, but the overwhelming majority are.... In every case, perpetrators view their victims as violating rules of religious conduct and act without remorse.

While the sample size is small, this study suggests that honor killing is accelerating in North America and may correlate with the numbers of first generation immigrants. The problem is diverse but originates with immigration from majority Muslim countries and regions—the Palestinian territories, the Kurdish regions of Turkey and Iraq, majority Muslim countries in the Balkans, Bangladesh, Egypt, and Afghanistan. Pakistanis account for the plurality. The common denominator in each case is not culture but religion.

In Both North America and Europe, family members conducted honor killings with excessive violence—repeatedly stabbing, raping, setting aflame, and bludgeoning—in more than half the cases.

Conflict of Cultural Moralities

The problem the West faces is complex. Muslims, Sikhs, and Hindus view honor and morality as a collective family matter. Rights are collective, not individual. Family, clan, and tribal rights supplant individual human rights.

In these groups, intellectuals and elites handicap the absorption of immigrants arriving from countries where honor is a communal virtue. For example, accusations of Islamophobia stymie discussion and policy formulation when policy makers seek to address problems occurring among Muslim immigrants. Still, there are legal interventions under way in Europe, home to between twenty and thirty million Muslim immigrants and their descendents, as opposed to perhaps four million in the United States and Canada. Honor-related violence is, therefore, more visible in Europe than in North America. In 2004, Sweden held an international conference on honor killing, calling for "international cooperation" on the issue. Conference participants concluded:

> Violence in the name of honor must be combated as an obstacle to women's enjoyment of human rights. Interpretations of honor as strongly connected with female chastity must be challenged. It can never be accepted that customs, traditions, or religious considerations are invoked to avoid obligations to eradicate violence against women and girls, including violence in the name of honor. Violence against women must be addressed from a rights-based perspective.... Measures should be taken in the areas of legislation, employment, education, and sexual and reproductive health and rights. Respect for women's enjoyment of human rights is intrinsically linked to democracy. International conventions must be incorporated into national legislation.

There have since been local conferences in England, France, and Germany. British law enforcement has begun to hide women in a program equivalent to the U.S. federal witness protection program. Great Britain has passed legislation to empower police to rescue British female citizens whose families have kidnapped and forcibly married them against their will, usually in Pakistan; the police will return them to Britain if the brides request it. There is a special police unit that deals with the forced, arranged marriages of children. A new movement has also arisen in England, "One Law for All. A Campaign Against Shari'a Law in Britain," launched by Maryam Namazie, an advocate opposed to honor killing and other honor-related violence. She has launched this movement to oppose the use of Shari'a courts because they discriminate against women. Additionally, schools in the Netherlands have been asked to be "more alert to honor violence," following research conducted for the Ministry of Integration.

The Situation in North America

U.S. law enforcement has made tremendous progress over the last forty years on issues related to violence against women. However, there are not yet any shelters for battered Muslim, Hindu, or Sikh girls or women who fear that they will be murdered for honor. A regular shelter for battered women does not specialize in honor killings, nor are there any provisions for foster families—Muslim or otherwise—who can protect girls targeted for murder by their biological families. Critics would oppose any such intervention, however, as a form of cultural oppression, for many victims may have to forfeit their identities in order to remain alive.

> *U.S. and Canadian immigration authorities.... should inform potential Muslim immigrants ... that honor killings are crimes, and that both murderers and their accomplices can and will be charged.*

It will be more difficult to save adult Muslim women from honor killing because an adult immigrant may not have any regular contact with people outside her immediate family. Only if she survives injuries that require medical attention will she have contact with strangers who may try to help her rescue herself.

Religious education may also be necessary. According to this study, 90 percent of honor murders in the West are committed by Muslims against Muslims. The perpetrators may interpret the Qur'an and Islam incorrectly, either for malicious reasons or simply because they are ignorant of more tolerant Muslim exegesis or conflate local customs with religion.

Here, Muslim-American and Muslim-Canadian associations might play a role so long as they cease obfuscation and recognize the religious roots of the problem. Now is the time for sheikhs in the United States and Canada to state without qualification that killing daughters, sisters, wives, and cousins is against Islam. A number of feminist lawyers who work with battered women have credited pro-women sheikhs with helping them enormously. Sheikhs should publicly identify, condemn, and shame honor killers. Those sheikhs who resist doing so should be challenged.

As with issues relating to terrorism, law enforcement and civil servants must be mindful of which Muslim community activists they seek to engage. Many self-described civil rights organizations—CAIR or the Islamic Society of North America, for example—lean towards more radical interpretations of Islam. Groups such as the American Islamic Congress and the American Islamic Forum for Democracy advocate for gender equality and human rights, but because their efforts against radicalism antagonize Saudi Arabia and other sources of funding, they often lack resources. Given alternative funding, they might be willing to assist in an effort to educate Muslims against honor murder.

U.S. and Canadian immigration authorities should also be aware of the issue. They should inform potential Muslim immigrants and new Muslim citizens that it is against the law to beat girls and women, that honor killings are crimes, and that both the murderers and their accomplices can and will be charged. Cultural equivalency will provide no excuse as it sometimes does in more permissive societies such as Great Britain and the Netherlands. As long as Islamist advocacy groups continue to obfuscate the problem, and government and police officials accept their inaccurate versions of reality, women will continue to be killed for honor in the West; such murders may even accelerate. Unchecked by Western law, their blood will be on society's hands.

VIEWPOINT 6

Jordan Cracks Down on Honor Killings

Tom Peter

Tom Peter reports on a change in the way honor killings are being handled in Jordanian courts. In the past, most men served short sentences for killing a woman whom he claimed had dishonored him. Now longer sentences are being handed down. Although honor killings continue to be a problem, Peter notes, many situations that might have led to murder are now being solved through other means. Some activists suggest this signals a change in overall attitudes and that honor killings will decrease as more people understand the consequences. Peter is a journalist who covers Jordan for the GlobalPost.

As you read, consider the following questions:

1. How much time in jail did a man who committed an honor killing generally serve in Jordan before 2010?
2. Who are the King and Queen of Jordan?
3. What do the longer prison sentences reflect, according to Enaam Asha?

For the first time [April 2010] after more than a decade of activism trying to stop so-called honor crimes, Rana Husseini says she doesn't have a lot to complain about in Jordan.

In the past, most men served less than a year for killing a woman who had "dishonored" her family. Now [2010] more

Tom Peter, "Jordon Honor Killings Draw Tough Response. Finally," Global Post, April 7, 2010. www.globalpost.com. Copyright © 2010 by Global Post. All rights reserved. Reproduced by permission.

Dowry Violence, Bride Burning, and Honor Killings

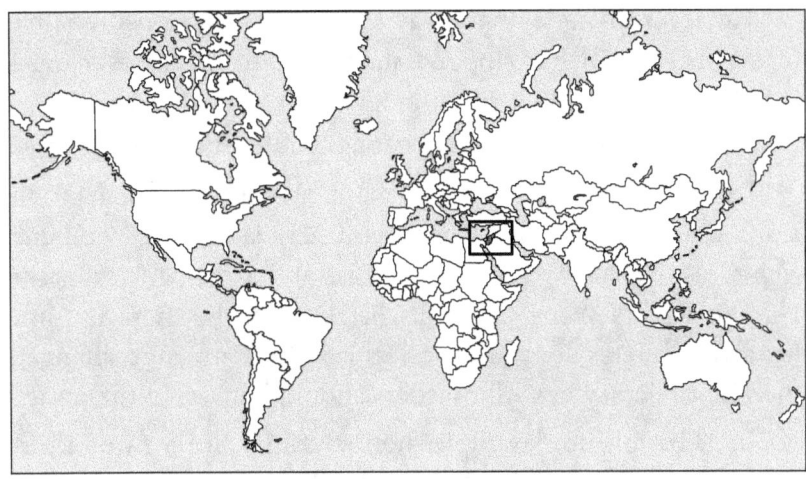

than seven months after the government restructured the legal system to deal with honor crimes as normal criminal cases, Jordan has seen at least 10 cases result in prison sentences of seven to 15 years.

The question remains: Are the days of convicted murderers receiving nominal three-month jail terms in Jordan over?

"Journalists used to come and interview me and I'd say we have to do this and we have to do that, but now I'm saying totally different things," said Husseini, author of *Murder in the Name of Honor* and a local journalist. "It's something very good, and it's about time."

More than seven months after the government restructured the legal system to deal with honor crimes as normal criminal cases, Jordan has seen at least 10 cases result in prison sentences of seven to 15 years.

A Huge Step Forward

The change is being heralded as a huge step forward for Jordan that could compel others in the region to take a tougher stance on honor crimes.

However, many activists say that while it's a positive turn of events, Jordan has stopped short of putting these changes into law. Without rewriting the law books, some worry that a new group of judges or other changes could undo the progress.

"Something really needs to happen with the legal provisions that are discriminatory," said Nadya Khalife, women's rights researcher for the Middle East and North Africa at the Human Rights Watch office in Beirut. "Maybe there is some headway, but as long as the legal aspects are not changed there's no victory yet. All murders should be treated the same."

In Lebanon, for example, honor crimes are a rare occurrence, but laws still exist that would allow perpetrators to face limited, if any, legal consequences for killing a woman in an honor crime. In Jordan, honor crimes remain a relatively limited occurrence, resulting in the death of about 20 people per year. Still, activists say that one is too many, especially if the murderer may be exempt from punishment.

After pressure from activist groups and even Jordan's King Abdullah II and Queen Rania, in July [2009] the courts created a special judicial committee to handle honor crimes. It also began working with nongovernmental organizations to educate legal officials about how to deal with the honor killings.

When these efforts began last summer, Husseini and many other activists doubted they would bring about much change. Since then, however, the court has yet to hand out one of the nominal prison sentences that used to be standard.

Still, in almost all honor crimes cases, families drop charges so the accused receive only half of the assigned prison sentence.

Attitudes Are Changing

"Here in Jordan, as a whole society there are some serious changes within the whole community about [attitudes] related

Honor Crimes in Jordan

Authorities prosecuted the 24 reported instances of homicides related to honor crimes that occurred during the year.... An Information and Research Center [of the King Hussein Foundation] study released on October 1 [2009] on the causes of honor crimes in the country showed a high correlation between poverty and education with honor crimes. The study found that 73 percent of victims since 2000 were classified as poor, a group that constituted only 30 percent of the country's population. The brother of the victim was the perpetrator in 76 percent of the cases and the father in 13 percent.

On July 28 [2009], the chief judge of the criminal courts announced the establishment of a special criminal court tribunal to hear all honor crime cases. In its first ruling on October 12, the tribunal issued a 15-year murder sentence to a 21-year-old man, convicted of stabbing and killing his married sister in the Jordan River Valley in 2008, because she allegedly slept with a man other than her husband. This sentence marked the first time a lower court issued a full murder sentence in an honor crime case without granting some form of leniency....

Prior to the tribunal's ruling, some lower courts handed down 15-year sentences for second-degree murder during the year; in every case the court immediately cut the sentence in half.... In previous years the courts usually found perpetrators of honor killings guilty of a "crime of passion," which merited a maximum sentence of three years. Although defendants were almost always found guilty, they often received token sentences of no more than six months. The maximum sentences for first- and second-degree murder are death and 15 years' imprisonment, respectively.

US Department of State, "2009 Human Rights Report: Jordan," March 11, 2010. www.state.gov.

to women's issues, even the judiciary system," said Ihssan Barakat, a judge in the court of appeals and chairwoman for the Arab Women's Legal Network. "They are accepting any new changes that give [women] better access to justice."

She said that despite the recent changes in how honor crimes were handled in Jordan, there had been no official modifications to the legal system. However, she was doubtful the system would see any backsliding to previous sentencing practices.

Though the overall number of honor crimes has not dropped, Enaam Asha, a member of the board of directors at the Sisterhood Is Global Institute in Jordan, said that her organization had begun to see a slight cultural shift in how people handled incidents that could have previously resulted in honor crimes.

Now, when a young woman had relations with a man before marriage, rather than escalating to violence, Asha said some families were willing to resolve the situation through nonviolent methods, such as marrying the couple. Additionally, she noted, the local media had begun reporting on honor crimes in such a way that was empathetic toward the victim. In the past, many news reports would condemn the murdered woman.

The longer prison sentences "reflect the change in the mentality of the judges in handling these kinds of cases and more importantly the change in the social perspective," Asha said. "Maybe the number of honor crimes is not decreasing ... but through our daily interaction with people working on this issue, we were able to spot that there is a difference in how people handle such issues. People are becoming more understanding to such cases, both on the perpetrator's part and the victim's part, and also the society and the families around them."

New Sentencing May Lead to Fewer Killings

Husseini and other activists hope that as word of the new sentencing procedure spreads, more people will continue to seek other means for resolving these situations and the number of honor killings may begin to fall.

"Men should know, the ones wanting to kill their female relatives, if they do kill them, they will end up spending a long time in prison," Husseini said.

Periodical and Internet Sources Bibliography

The following articles have been selected to supplement the diverse views presented in this chapter.

Yasmin Alibhai-Brown	"Wicked Mothers-in-Law Destroy Lives," *Independent*, June 1, 2009, p. 26.
Akhtar Amin	"90 Honour Killings Reported in First Quarter of 2008," *Daily Times* (Pakistan), September 20, 2008. www.dailytimes.com.pk.
Lucy Ballinger	"Honour Kill Girl, 15, 'Was Pregnant': Muslim Father Gets Life for Murdering Daughter Who Fell in Love with the Wrong Man," *Mail Online*, December 18, 2009. www.dailymail.co.uk.
Phyllis Chesler	"Worldwide Trends in Honor Killings," *Middle East Quarterly*, vol. 18, no. 2, Spring 2010, pp. 3–11. www.meforum.org.
Tracy McVeigh and Tara Sutton	"Girls Undergo Horror of Genital Mutilation Despite Tough Laws," *Observer*, July 25, 2010, p. 20.
CT Nilesh	"Bride Burning: Another Chapter on the Humiliation of the Indian Woman," AsiaNews.it, June 15, 2009. www.asianews.it.
Abigail Pesta	"An American Honor Killing," *Marie Claire*, July 8, 2010. www.marieclaire.com.
Navi Pillay	"Five Thousand Women Are Murdered by Family Yearly," *New Vision* (Uganda), March 9, 2010. www.newvision.co.ug.
J. Venkatesan	"Dowry Killings Deserve Death Penalty: Supreme Court," *Hindu* (New Delhi), October 31, 2010. www.thehindu.com.

CHAPTER 3

Family Violence and Children

VIEWPOINT 1

In China and Other Asian Countries, Girl Babies Are the Victims of Family Violence

The Economist

According to the following viewpoint, in countries such as China, Taiwan, India, South Korea, and Singapore, sex ratios at birth are heavily skewed toward male babies. This is largely because families there prefer boy babies and use modern screening technologies to identify and abort girl babies. In addition, asserts the Economist, *girl babies are much less likely to survive infancy and childhood in these countries. This imbalance is likely to have far-reaching implications globally. The* Economist *is an international newspaper.*

As you read, consider the following questions:

1. What are the so-called "bare branches" referred to in this viewpoint?
2. What percentage of Korean marriages in 2008 were between a Korean man and a foreign woman?
3. What Hindu saying about raising a daughter does the viewpoint quote?

The Economist, "The Worldwide War on Baby Girls," March 4, 2010. www.economist.com. Copyright © 2010 by *The Economist*. All rights reserved. Reproduced by permission.

Family Violence and Children

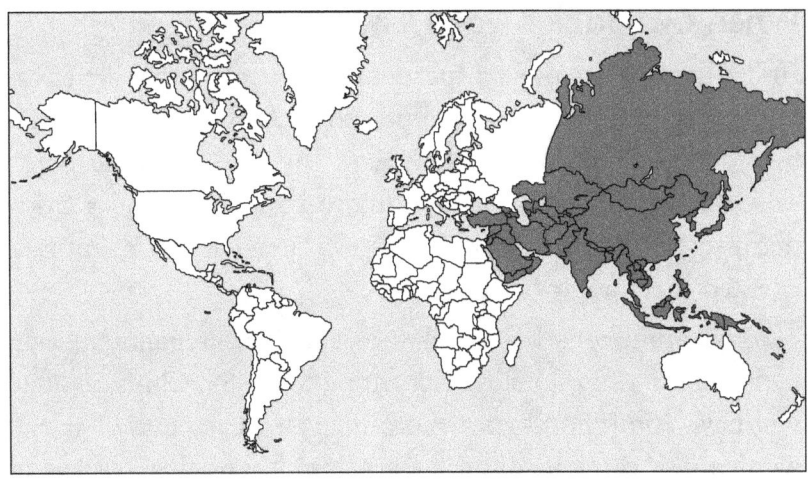

Xinran Xue, a Chinese writer, describes visiting a peasant family in the Yimeng area of Shandong province. The wife was giving birth. "We had scarcely sat down in the kitchen", she writes, "when we heard a moan of pain from the bedroom next door.... The cries from the inner room grew louder—and abruptly stopped. There was a low sob, and then a man's gruff voice said accusingly: 'Useless thing!'

"Suddenly, I thought I heard a slight movement in the slops pail behind me," Miss Xinran remembers. "To my absolute horror, I saw a tiny foot poking out of the pail. The midwife must have dropped that tiny baby alive into the slops pail! I nearly threw myself at it, but the two policemen [who had accompanied me] held my shoulders in a firm grip. 'Don't move, you can't save it, it's too late.'

"'But that's ... murder ... and you're the police!' The little foot was still now. The policemen held on to me for a few more minutes. 'Doing a baby girl is not a big thing around here,' [an] older woman said comfortingly. 'That's a living child,' I said in a shaking voice, pointing at the slops pail. 'It's not a child,' she corrected me. 'It's a girl baby, and we can't keep it. Around these parts, you can't get by without a son. Girl babies don't count.'"

Family Violence

When Girl Babies Don't Count

In January 2010 the Chinese Academy of Social Sciences (CASS) showed what can happen to a country when girl babies don't count. Within ten years [by 2020], the academy said, one in five young men would be unable to find a bride because of the dearth of young women—a figure unprecedented in a country at peace.

The number is based on the sexual discrepancy among people aged 19 and below. According to CASS, China in 2020 will have 30m[illion]–40m more men of this age than young women. For comparison, there are 23m boys below the age of 20 in Germany, France and Britain combined and around 40m American boys and young men. So within ten years, China faces the prospect of having the equivalent of the whole young male population of America, or almost twice that of Europe's three largest countries, with little prospect of marriage, untethered to a home of their own and without the stake in society that marriage and children provide.

[By 2020] . . . one in five young men would be unable to find a bride because of the dearth of young women—a figure unprecedented in a country at peace.

Gendercide—to borrow the title of a 1985 book by Mary Anne Warren—is often seen as an unintended consequence of China's one-child policy, or as a product of poverty or ignorance. But that cannot be the whole story. The surplus of bachelors—called in China *guanggun*, or "bare branches"—seems to have accelerated between 1990 and 2005, in ways not obviously linked to the one-child policy, which was introduced in 1979. And, as is becoming clear, the war against baby girls is not confined to China.

The Selective Destruction of Baby Girls

Parts of India have sex ratios as skewed as anything in its northern neighbour. Other East Asian countries—South Korea, Singapore and Taiwan—have peculiarly high numbers of male births. So, since the collapse of the Soviet Union, have former Communist countries in the Caucasus and the western Balkans. Even subsets of America's population are following suit, though not the population as a whole.

The real cause, argues Nick Eberstadt, a demographer at the American Enterprise Institute, a think tank in Washington, DC, is not any country's particular policy but "the fateful collision between overweening son preference, the use of rapidly spreading prenatal sex-determination technology and declining fertility." These are global trends. And the selective destruction of baby girls is global, too.

Boys are slightly more likely to die in infancy than girls. To compensate, more boys are born than girls so there will be equal numbers of young men and women at puberty. In all societies that record births, between 103 and 106 boys are normally born for every 100 girls. The ratio has been so stable over time that it appears to be the natural order of things.

A Growing Gender Imbalance

That order has changed fundamentally in the past 25 years. In China the sex ratio for the generation born between 1985 and 1989 was 108, already just outside the natural range. For the generation born in 2000–04, it was 124 (i.e., 124 boys were born in those years for every 100 girls). According to CASS the ratio today is 123 boys per 100 girls. These rates are biologically impossible without human intervention.

The national averages hide astonishing figures at the provincial level. According to an analysis of Chinese household data carried out in late 2005 and reported in the *British Medical Journal* [BMJ], only one region, Tibet, has a sex ratio within the bounds of nature. Fourteen provinces—mostly in the east and south—have sex ratios at birth of 120 and above, and three have unprecedented levels of more than 130. As CASS says, "the gender imbalance has been growing wider year after year."

The BMJ study also casts light on one of the puzzles about China's sexual imbalance. How far has it been exaggerated by the presumed practice of not reporting the birth of baby daughters in the hope of getting another shot at bearing a son? Not much, the authors think. If this explanation were correct, you would expect to find sex ratios falling precipitously as girls who had been hidden at birth start entering the official registers on attending school or the doctor. In fact, there is no such fall. The sex ratio of 15-year-olds in 2005 was not far from the sex ratio at birth in 1990. The implication is that sex-selective abortion, not under-registration of girls, accounts for the excess of boys.

Other countries have wildly skewed sex ratios without China's draconian population controls. Taiwan's sex ratio also rose from just above normal in 1980 to 110 in the early 1990s; it remains just below that level today. During the same period, South Korea's sex ratio rose from just above normal to 117 in 1990—then the highest in the world—before falling back to more natural levels. Both these countries were already rich, growing quickly and becoming more highly educated even while the balance between the sexes was swinging sharply towards males.

The implication is that sex-selective abortion, not under-registration of girls, accounts for the excess of boys.

South Korea is experiencing some surprising consequences. The surplus of bachelors in a rich country has sucked in brides from abroad. In 2008, 11% of marriages were "mixed", mostly between a Korean man and a foreign woman. This is causing tensions in a hitherto homogenous society, which is

Family Violence and Children

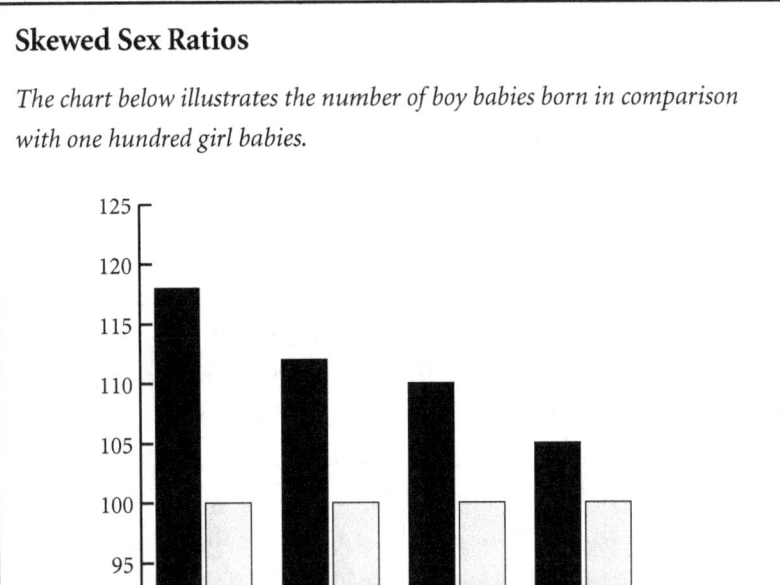

Skewed Sex Ratios

The chart below illustrates the number of boy babies born in comparison with one hundred girl babies.

TAKEN FROM: Based on data from The World Factbook, 2009.

often hostile to the children of mixed marriages. The trend is especially marked in rural areas, where the government thinks half the children of farm households will be mixed by 2020. The children are common enough to have produced a new word: "Kosians", or Korean-Asians.

Distorted Sex Ratios in Many Countries

China is nominally a Communist country, but elsewhere it was communism's collapse that was associated with the growth of sexual disparities. After the Soviet Union imploded in 1991, there was an upsurge in the ratio of boys to girls in Armenia, Azerbaijan and Georgia. Their sex ratios rose from normal levels in 1991 to 115–120 by 2000. A rise also occurred in several Balkan states after the wars of Yugoslav succession. The ratio in Serbia and Macedonia is around 108. There are even signs of distorted sex ratios in America, among various groups of Asian-Americans. In 1975, calculates Mr Eberstadt, the sex ratio for Chinese-, Japanese- and Filipino-Americans was between 100 and 106. In 2002, it was 107 to 109.

But the country with the most remarkable record is that other supergiant, India. India does not produce figures for sex ratios at birth, so its numbers are not strictly comparable with the others. But there is no doubt that the number of boys has been rising relative to girls and that, as in China, there are large regional disparities. The northwestern states of Punjab and Haryana have sex ratios as high as the provinces of China's east and south. Nationally, the ratio for children up to six years of age rose from a biologically unexceptionable 104 in 1981 to a biologically impossible 108 in 2001. In 1991, there was a single district with a sex ratio over 125; by 2001, there were 46.

Conventional wisdom about such disparities is that they are the result of "backward thinking" in old-fashioned societies or—in China—of the one-child policy. By implication, reforming the policy or modernising the society (by, for example, enhancing the status of women) should bring the sex ratio back to normal. But this is not always true and, where it is, the road to normal sex ratios is winding and bumpy.

In Punjab [India] ... second and third daughters of well-educated mothers were more than twice as likely to die before their fifth birthday as their brothers, regardless of their birth order.

Not all traditional societies show a marked preference for sons over daughters. But in those that do—especially those in which the family line passes through the son and in which he is supposed to look after his parents in old age—a son is worth more than a daughter. A girl is deemed to have joined her husband's family on marriage, and is lost to her parents. As a Hindu saying puts it, "Raising a daughter is like watering your neighbours' garden."

"Son preference" is discernible—overwhelming, even—in polling evidence. In 1999 the government of India asked women what sex they wanted their next child to be. One-third of those without children said a son, two-thirds had no preference and only a residual said a daughter. Polls carried out in Pakistan and Yemen show similar results. Mothers in some developing countries say they want sons, not daughters, by margins of ten to one. In China midwives charge more for delivering a son than a daughter. . . .

In Punjab Monica Das Gupta of the World Bank discovered that second and third daughters of well-educated mothers were more than twice as likely to die before their fifth birthday as their brothers, regardless of their birth order. The discrepancy was far lower in poorer households. Ms Das Gupta argues that women do not necessarily use improvements in education and income to help daughters. Richer, well-educated families share their poorer neighbours' preference for sons and, because they tend to have smaller families, come under greater pressure to produce a son and heir if their first child is an unlooked-for daughter.

VIEWPOINT 2

The World Health Organization Calls for the Elimination of Female Genital Mutilation

The World Health Organization

The World Health Organization (WHO), the public health arm of the United Nations, believes that female genital mutilation (FGM) must cease in all countries. FGM is a cultural, social, and religious custom in many parts of the world. WHO views FGM as a violation of the rights of women and girls. The procedure is performed primarily on young girls under the age of fifteen at the insistence of their families in order to make her less likely to be sexually active. The consequences of the procedure are severe and long lasting.

As you read, consider the following questions:

1. What specific rights does WHO say female genital mutilation violates?
2. What are some of the specific long-term consequences of female genital mutilation listed by WHO in this viewpoint?
3. On what do WHO efforts to eliminate female genital mutilation focus?

World Health Organization, "Female Genital Mutilation," Fact Sheet no. 241, February 2010. www.who.int/mediacentre/factsheets/fs241/en. Copyright © 2010 by the World Health Organization. All rights reserved. Reproduced by permission.

Key Facts

- Female genital mutilation (FGM) includes procedures that intentionally alter or injure female genital organs for nonmedical reasons.

- The procedure has no health benefits for girls and women.

- Procedures can cause severe bleeding and problems urinating, and later, potential childbirth complications and newborn deaths.

- An estimated 100 to 140 million girls and women worldwide are currently living with the consequences of FGM.

- It is mostly carried out on young girls sometime between infancy and age 15 years.

- In Africa an estimated 92 million girls from 10 years of age and above have undergone FGM.

- FGM is internationally recognized as a violation of the human rights of girls and women.

Female genital mutilation (FGM) comprises all procedures that involve partial or total removal of the external female genitalia, or other injury to the female genital organs for nonmedical reasons.

The practice is mostly carried out by traditional circumcisers, who often play other central roles in communities, such as attending childbirths. Increasingly, however, FGM is being performed by health care providers.

FGM is recognized internationally as a violation of the human rights of girls and women. It reflects deep-rooted inequality between the sexes, and constitutes an extreme form of discrimination against women. It is nearly always carried out on minors and is a violation of the rights of children. The practice also violates a person's rights to health, security and physical integrity, the right to be free from torture and cruel, inhuman or degrading treatment, and the right to life when the procedure results in death.

The practice [FGM] is mostly carried out by traditional circumcisers, who often play other central roles in communities, such as attending childbirths. Increasingly, however, FGM is being performed by health care providers.

Procedures

Female genital mutilation is classified into four major types.

1. Clitoridectomy: partial or total removal of the clitoris (a small, sensitive and erectile part of the female genitals) and, in very rare cases, only the prepuce (the fold of skin surrounding the clitoris).
2. Excision: partial or total removal of the clitoris and the labia minora, with or without excision of the labia majora (the labia are "the lips" that surround the vagina).
3. Infibulation: narrowing of the vaginal opening through the creation of a covering seal. The seal is formed by cutting and repositioning the inner, or outer, labia, with or without removal of the clitoris.
4. Other: all other harmful procedures to the female genitalia for nonmedical purposes, e.g., pricking, piercing, incising, scraping and cauterizing the genital area.

No Health Benefits, Only Harm

FGM has no health benefits, and it harms girls and women in many ways. It involves removing and damaging healthy and normal female genital tissue, and interferes with the natural functions of girls' and women's bodies.

Immediate complications can include severe pain, shock, haemorrhage (bleeding), tetanus or sepsis (bacterial infection), urine retention, open sores in the genital region and injury to nearby genital tissue.

FGM has no health benefits, and it harms girls and women in many ways.

Long-term consequences can include:

- recurrent bladder and urinary tract infections;
- cysts;
- infertility;
- an increased risk of childbirth complications and newborn deaths;
- the need for later surgeries. For example, the FGM procedure that seals or narrows a vaginal opening (type 3 above) needs to be cut open later to allow for sexual intercourse and childbirth. Sometimes it is stitched again several times, including after childbirth, hence the woman goes through repeated opening and closing procedures, further increasing and repeated both immediate and long-term risks.

Who Is at Risk?

Procedures are mostly carried out on young girls sometime between infancy and age 15, and occasionally on adult women. In Africa, about three million girls are at risk for FGM annually.

Between 100 to 140 million girls and women worldwide are living with the consequences of FGM. In Africa, about 92 million girls age 10 years and above are estimated to have undergone FGM.

Family Violence

The practice is most common in the western, eastern, and northeastern regions of Africa, in some countries in Asia and the Middle East, and among certain immigrant communities in North America and Europe.

Between 100 to 140 million girls and women worldwide are living with the consequences of FGM.

Cultural, Religious and Social Causes

The causes of female genital mutilation include a mix of cultural, religious and social factors within families and communities.

- Where FGM is a social convention, the social pressure to conform to what others do and have been doing is a strong motivation to perpetuate the practice.

- FGM is often considered a necessary part of raising a girl properly, and a way to prepare her for adulthood and marriage.

- FGM is often motivated by beliefs about what is considered proper sexual behaviour, linking procedures to premarital virginity and marital fidelity. FGM is in many communities believed to reduce a woman's libido, and thereby is further believed to help her resist "illicit" sexual acts. When a vaginal opening is covered or narrowed (type 3 above), the fear of pain of opening it, and the fear that this will be found out, is expected to further discourage "illicit" sexual intercourse among women with this type of FGM.

- FGM is associated with cultural ideals of femininity and modesty, which include the notion that girls are "clean" and "beautiful" after removal of body parts that are considered "male" or "unclean".

Family Violence and Children

Percentage of Women Who Have Undergone Female Genital Mutilation, by African Country

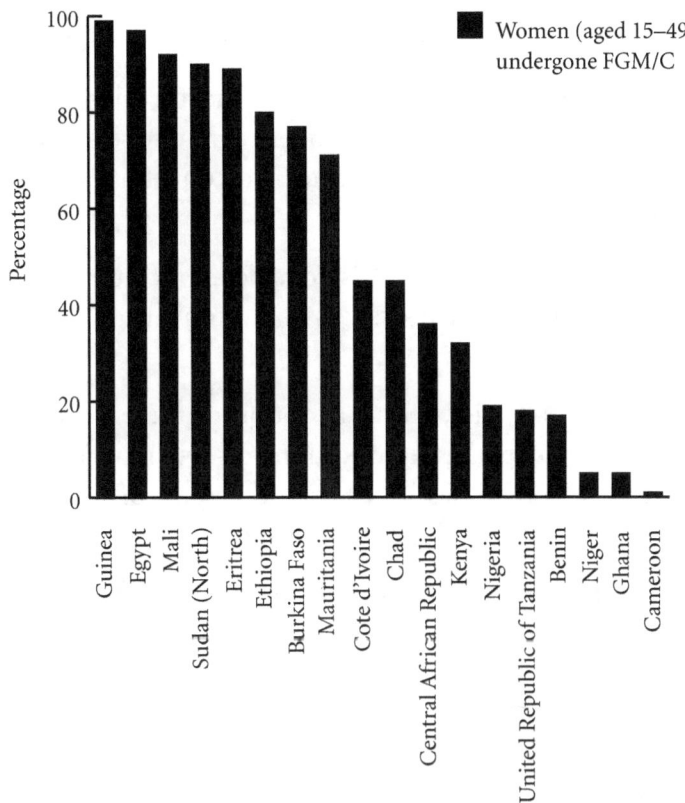

The most reliable and extensive data on prevalence and nature of FGM [female genital multilation] are provided by DHS [Demographic and Health Surveys] and MICS [Multiple Indicator Cluster Surveys]. However, the surveys do not capture the degree of severity of mutilation, which varies considerably between and within countries. In addition, some of the countries in which FGM is known to be most frequently practised, such as Somalia and Djibouti, have not been subject to these surveys.

TAKEN FROM: United Nations, *World Report on Violence Against Children*, 2006.

- Though no religious scripts prescribe the practice, practitioners often believe the practice has religious support.

- Religious leaders take varying positions with regard to FGM: some promote it, some consider it irrelevant to religion, and others contribute to its elimination.

- Local structures of power and authority, such as community leaders, religious leaders, circumcisers, and even some medical personnel can contribute to upholding the practice.

- In most societies, FGM is considered a cultural tradition, which is often used as an argument for its continuation.

- In some societies, recent adoption of the practice is linked to copying the traditions of neighbouring groups. Sometimes it has started as part of a wider religious or traditional revival movement.

- In some societies, FGM is being practised by new groups when they move into areas where the local population practice FGM.

International Response

In 1997, the World Health Organization (WHO) issued a joint statement with the United Nations Children's Fund (UNICEF) and the United Nations Population Fund (UNFPA) against the practice of FGM. A new statement, with wider United Nations support, was then issued in February 2008 to support increased advocacy for the abandonment of FGM.

The 2008 statement documents new evidence collected over the past decade about the practice. It highlights the increased recognition of the human rights and legal dimensions of the problem and provides current data on the frequency and scope of FGM. It also summarizes research about why

Family Violence and Children

FGM continues, how to stop it, and its damaging effects on the health of women, girls and newborn babies.

Since 1997, great efforts have been made to counteract FGM, through research, work within communities, and changes in public policy. Progress at both international and local levels includes:

- wider international involvement to stop FGM;
- the development of international monitoring bodies and resolutions that condemn the practice;
- revised legal frameworks and growing political support to end FGM; and
- in some countries, decreasing practice of FGM, and an increasing number of women and men in practising communities who declare their support to end it.

Research shows that, if practising communities themselves decide to abandon FGM, the practice can be eliminated very rapidly.

WHO Response

In 2008, the World Health Assembly passed a resolution (WHA61.16) on the elimination of FGM, emphasizing the need for concerted action in all sectors—health, education, finance, justice and women's affairs.

WHO efforts to eliminate female genital mutilation focus on:

- advocacy: developing publications and advocacy tools for international, regional and local efforts to end FGM within a generation;
- research: generating knowledge about the causes and consequences of the practice, how to eliminate it, and how to care for those who have experienced FGM;

- guidance for health systems: developing training materials and guidelines for health professionals to help them treat and counsel women who have undergone procedures.

WHO is particularly concerned about the increasing trend for medically trained personnel to perform FGM. WHO strongly urges health professionals not to perform such procedures.

VIEWPOINT 3

In Uganda, the Practice of Female Genital Mutilation Continues Despite the Law

Frederick Womakuyu

According to the following viewpoint, elders of the Sabiny tribe of Uganda continue to practice female circumcision, also called female genital mutilation (FGM), on young girls, despite laws passed in 2010 banning the custom. The author reports that men like their wives to be circumcised because it makes them less interested in sex and less likely to betray them with another man. Many of the girls go through the procedure of their own choice due to cultural pressure. Frederick Womakuyu is a staff features writer for Vision Group in Uganda.

As you read, consider the following questions:

1. What Ugandan president signed the law banning female circumcision in his country, and when did he sign it?
2. From what grains is the local brew Malwa made?
3. What is the punishment for someone who carries out female genital mutilation?

Elders in Bukwo and Kapchorwa [Uganda] districts are preparing to circumcise over 200 girls next month [December 2010] despite a new law banning the practice. They swear that the whole tribe would rather go to prison than abolish a custom they inherited from their ancestors.

Frederick Womakuyu, "To Hell with the Law! We Shall Circumcise the Girls," *New Vision* (Kampala), November 5, 2010. Copyright © 2010 by New Vision Print and Publishing. All rights reserved. Reproduced by permission.

Family Violence

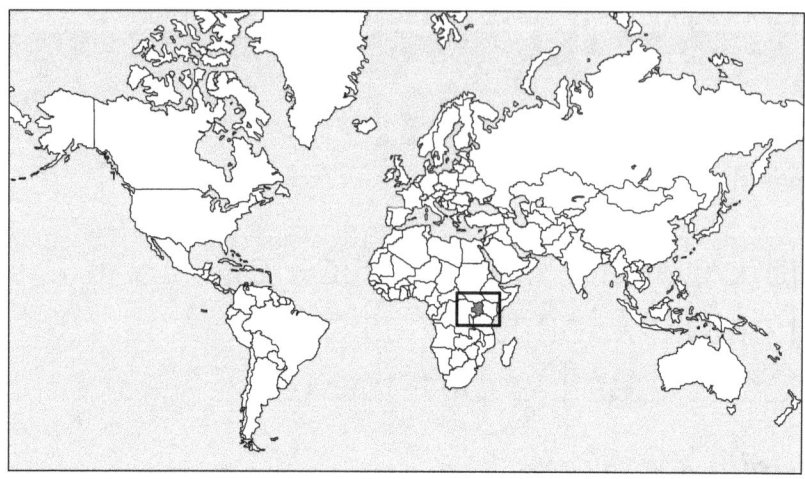

The practice, commonly referred to as female circumcision, is mostly practiced among the Sabiny, who occupy Bukwo and Kapchorwa districts on the northern slopes of Mt Elgon. The United Nations categorises it as female genital mutilation (FGM) because it damages a woman's sexuality and leads to various complications. FGM refers to the removal of the external female genitalia.

FGM Is Outlawed

Accordingly, last December Parliament passed a law banning female circumcision. President Yoweri Museveni signed it into law on March 17, 2010, and it took effect on April 9, 2010.

The law argues that FGM infringes on the rights of the woman and also leads to health hazards, including excessive bleeding, death, birth complications and exposure to illnesses. The law criminalises the practice, calls for prosecution of offenders and protection of victims. Anyone caught doing it faces 10 years in jail or life imprisonment if the victim dies.

But the Sabiny are unfazed by this law. The vice-chairman of Bukwo district, John Chelangat, says over 200 girls are being prepared for the practice beginning on December 1 and neither he nor other political leaders are able to stop it. The

Family Violence and Children

men like it because circumcised women are less interested in sex and are, therefore, less likely to have extramarital affairs. The girls do not want to be considered outcasts, so they go for the knife.

"This is a very sensitive period and no politician will talk about abolishing FGM because we shall lose votes. Myself, I will not talk about FGM because I know this will land me into the political dustbin," says Chelangat.

Consequently, as the December 1, 2010, circumcision nears, preparations to grace the ritual are in high gear in Sebei region.

In Bukwo district, the residents had a bumper harvest of maize, sorghum and millet that is being used for making local brew (Malwa) to entertain the revelers and also aid in performing sacred rituals, only known to the Sabiny people.

The Community Refuses to Obey the Law

Kokop Chebet, 70, a mentor from Matibeyi village in Suam sub-county-Bukwo, says she has received applications from over 20 girls wishing to be prepared for the ritual.

"They came to me in January and I have been training them on how to go through the ritual. They told me they want to become women like others because they are tired of being scolded by the community that still calls them girls because they are not cut," she adds.

Alice Kokop, 65, another mentor from Suam says she has also received about 15 applications from girls in Kabei sub-county wishing to be cut.

Other girls are to come from Chesower and Bukwo town council sub-counties. "I have already taken them through a series of trainings and they are about to be ready. We shall cut the first group in the first week of December," Kokop explains.

Asked about the law prohibiting FGM, the two said a law cannot stop the cultural rite of the Sabiny people unless the community agrees with it.

> ## The Ritual of Female Genital Mutilation
>
> Some cried. Some were confused. Others still traumatised, while many were left speechless. They looked on in disbelief as a local female surgeon tried in vain thrice, probably using a very blunt knife, to cut off a girl's clitoris.
>
> She then asked for another, similarly blunt knife and to make it work, applied extra force, going back and forth, the way a saw cuts into timber. The girl struggled not to show fear and to contain her trembling, which is culturally unacceptable and would have attracted scorn and ridicule from the attentive crowd.
>
> "Uganda: 120 Sabiny Girls Circumcised,"
> New Vision *(Kampala),*
> December 3, 2010.

Twenty-year-old Ana Chebet is a resident of Matibeyi village in Suam. Married with three children, Chebet has always been scolded by the community for not undergoing circumcision that passes her from childhood to adulthood.

"I cannot milk a cow or climb into the family granary. Whenever I go to the well, other women throw scorn at me because I am not cut," adds Chebet, who will be one of the candidates this December.

She says mentors trained her how to dance when preparing for the ritual, the kind of food to eat, including posho, beans, honey and fermented milk to replace lost energy and blood.

Some Women Refuse

Alice Chemutai, 17, another resident of Matibeyi, was convinced by her aunt to undergo female circumcision. But because she is educated she refused and her father supported her.

Family Violence and Children

She recites an endless list of young girls who have dropped out of school to get married after the ritual and those who have had birth complications, bleeding and infections after.

"I will never get circumcised because this will not only infringe on my rights of womanhood but will also expose me to long-term health hazards. I am happy my father and mother support me against other relatives," adds Chemutai, a Senior Three student at Amananga High School in Suam.

According to the law, a person commits aggravated FGM in situations where death occurs or where the victim is disabled or is infected with HIV/AIDS.

A person also commits aggravated FGM where the offender is a parent, guardian or person having control over the victim or where the act is done by a health worker.

According to Sabiny customs and traditions, female circumcision has been around for over 2,000 years and it is carried out to convert a female from childhood to adulthood.

The law punishes a person who commits aggravated FGM with life imprisonment.

A person who carries out FGM shall be imprisoned for a period not exceeding 10 years. People who participate or aid FGM shall be jailed.

The Sabiny people claim they do not fear the law and they are ready to die for FGM. "This law was not initiated or brought by the people of Sebei. It was brought by the people who do not understand why we carry out circumcision," adds Alice Kokop.

According to Sabiny customs and traditions, female circumcision has been around for over 2,000 years and it is carried out to convert a female from childhood to adulthood. Females who are not circumcised are not called women and they are not supposed to carry out certain home activities like milking a cow, climbing into a family granary and talking with the elders.

VIEWPOINT 4

Female Genital Mutilation Is Practiced in Parts of Europe

Laura Schweiger

Although Africa leads the world in the practice of female genital mutilation (FGM), many European girls and women are also victims of the practice, according to Laura Schweiger. Girls travel with their parents to the parents' homeland and are often subjected to FGM before returning to Europe. Women who have had FGM performed on them need extensive aftercare and lifelong health support. Groups such as Amnesty International urge the European Union to provide this care. Schweiger is a German journalist who writes for Deutsche Welle, Germany's international broadcaster.

As you read, consider the following questions:

1. How many women in the United Kingdom, Germany, and France, respectively, have already been subjected to FGM or are in danger of becoming victims?
2. Where did FGM victim Aissatou Diallo find her footing in Europe?
3. For what purpose is Shewa Sium collecting signatures for a petition?

Practiced in Africa as well as in certain countries in the Middle East and communities in Asia and Latin America, female genital mutilation [FGM] is the internationally ac-

Laura Schweiger, "Female Genital Mutilation Is Also an Issue in Europe, Say Activists," *Deutsche Welle*, November 25, 2010. Copyright © 2010 by Al Bawaba Ltd. All rights reserved. Reproduced by permission.

Family Violence

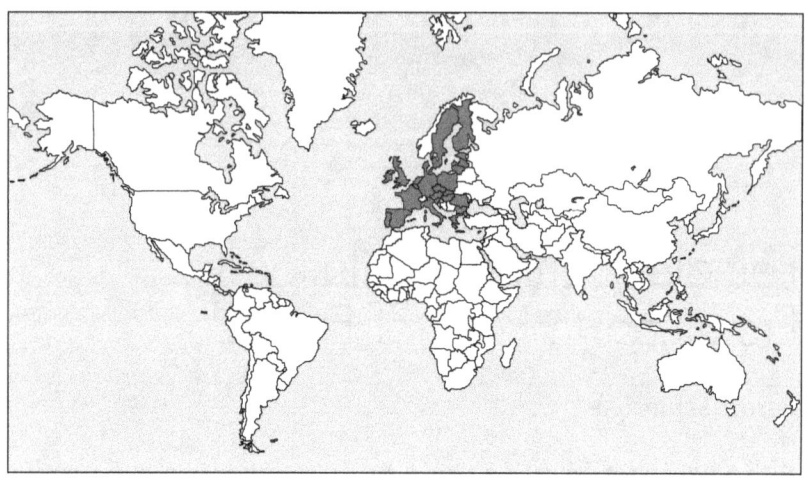

knowledged name for the practice of cutting women's genitalia. Girls are subjected to FGM for a variety of reasons, explained Christine Loudes, director of the End FGM campaign at Amnesty International.

"FGM is performed for nontherapeutic reasons," Loudes said. "It's done in the name of tradition, in the name of aesthetics and sometimes in the name of religion."

FGM involves partially or completely removing the external female genitalia, and the practice is usually performed under unhygienic conditions and without anaesthesia on girls from their birth to 15 years of age. FGM represents a severe violation of human rights.

"It constitutes torture and degrading treatment; it violates women's rights, and it violates rights to physical integrity as well as to children's rights, to name a few," Loudes added.

FGM Is Practiced Worldwide

Africa is the most notable perpetrator regarding FGM, with some 30 countries subjecting girls to the practice. But girls are threatened by the practice on other continents as well. According to the European Parliament, roughly 500,000 girls and women in Europe have already been subjected to FGM or are in danger of becoming victims. That number includes 75,000 girls and women in the UK [United Kingdom], 65,000 in France and 30,000 in Germany. As Loudes explains, it's difficult to prove that FGM is actually being carried out on the ground in Europe, but Amnesty International does not want to rule out the possibility.

"I cannot say that it's hard evidence. There's anecdotal evidence that this is done in Europe and that actually there is a cross-border dimension to it," Loudes said. "But mostly we know that it's happening when girls are going with their parents on holiday to their parents' country of origin, and that's where they are most at risk."

One FGM victim living in Europe is Aissatou Diallo, a native of Guinea who was mutilated in her home country at the age of 14. Fearing that her own daughters might meet the same fate, the family came to Belgium in 2007 as refugees. Diallo says she now lives with a sense of security.

According to the European Parliament, roughly 500,000 girls and women in Europe have already been subjected to FGM or are in danger of becoming victims.

"I've noticed that since coming to Belgium I've had peace of mind, because my children go to school and they are safe here," Diallo said. "I don't come home and ask, 'Where are my girls? Did someone take them away to cut them?', which is what often happens in my country. So here I've been able to enjoy life again, and I've learned to rebuild myself psychologically."

Diallo may have found her footing in Belgium, but Christine Loudes says that the recovery process is long and demanding for FGM victims who arrive in Europe.

"They need a lot of health care support," she stressed. "In particular, some form of reparation is required for women whose vagina has been stitched together. These women will need to be unstitched and they will need psychological support because it's a practice that brings a lot of psychological and physical trauma."

Victims Need Health Care

Run by Amnesty International in coordination with nongovernment organizations in 11 different European countries, the End FGM campaign has set accessible health care for FGM victims living in Europe as a priority. In Germany, for example, there is still work to be done in achieving this goal.

"The treatment and the operations needed for FGM victims are not covered by health insurance here," explained Shewa Sium, director of the Cologne-based refugee support organization agisra. "The women have to pay for it themselves. Right now, we're collecting signatures for a petition so that medical treatment for victims of FGM can also be covered by insurance companies."

But it's not just the FGM victims who need support. Organizations like Amnesty International and agisra are calling on EU [European Union] member states to give government workers the resources and training they need to tackle an issue they are unlikely to have encountered before.

Health Professionals Need Training

"We hear a lot of health professionals, teachers and social workers are confronted with the practice, and they don't know how to deal with the situation," said Christine Loudes. "The most difficult moment is at the time of giving birth, during which there is a lot of risk for the mother and the baby. The fact that health professionals are not used to dealing with women who have undergone FGM means that there is often an emergency caesarean section. This leads to increased costs in the health system as well as a higher risk for the women."

Because FGM has a lifelong physical and psychological impact on its victims, organizations like Amnesty International also emphasize the need to protect girls and women at risk, often via asylum in Europe. The European Union, however, lacks unified procedures and legislation when it comes to FGM.

"What is problematic is that each member state has a very different approach in relation to FGM," explains Loudes. "In some cases it is recognized as persecution, and in other cases you get another status that is less protective and is only temporary. In some countries, the level of awareness is very low, in particular in the new countries that have joined the EU. We are trying to change this by providing some education to asylum officers."

> FGM has a lifelong physical and psychological impact on its victims.

The EU Prioritizes Ending FGM

In an effort to achieve a streamlined, forceful approach against FGM from EU member states, the European Commission is also taking steps. Viviane Reding, the justice and fundamental rights commissioner, has flagged FGM as an issue in a five-year strategy for equality between women and men, and the Commission may further target FGM in a new policy paper due out in February 2011.

"The Commission is going to come out with a strategy policy paper on violence in general and victims. FGM is one of the priorities for the commission," said Matthew Newman, spokesperson for Commissioner Reding.

"It's possible that we will include it in the victims' strategy. It's a horrible practice, and people need to know that. They also need to know that the European Union is working with member states to raise awareness and doing everything we can to stop it."

While the EU's efforts are welcome news for women like Aissatou Diallo, she cautions that European countries and their citizens must also treat the issue of FGM with sensitivity to avoid stigmatizing its victims.

"When we talk about terrible things that others don't understand, we simply need to tell them: it's as if you would take a child in Europe and cut off an ear, an arm, or an eye. The child has been mutilated; it's as simple as that," she explained.

"It's true that we're not seen as complete women. We're seen as handicapped, almost. But we are people like you, and as Africans, we are fighting for change. Our hope is to be the last women in the world who have suffered from this practice."

VIEWPOINT 5

Divorce Can Lead to Violence Directed at Children

Graeme Hamilton

Canadian journalist Graeme Hamilton reports on the case of Danyela and Deyan Perisic, two children who were shot by their father rather than allowing the children to live with their mother. Although the children had spent nearly their whole lives in Canada, they were sent to Texas to live with their father on a Canadian judge's ruling based on a legal framework that deals with international child abduction. When a Texas judge ruled that the children should be returned to Canada, Perisic shot them both rather than comply. Deyan was killed while Danyela survived.

As you read, consider the following questions:

1. Why did Predrag Perisic move to Texas from Montreal?
2. How old is the Hague convention dealing with international child abduction, according to the viewpoint?
3. What was the name of the Quebec Superior Court Justice who granted Ms. Vucerakovich (the children's mother) custody and ordered them returned to Canada?

Graeme Hamilton, "Children Caught in the Middle; Montreal Family's Custody Battle Takes Deadly Turn," *National Post* (Canada), December 16, 2010, p. A1. Copyright © 2010 by *National Post*. All rights reserved. Material reproduced with the express permission of National Post Inc.

When Danyela and Deyan Perisic testified during their parents' custody dispute in Quebec Superior Court last April [2010], they made it clear they wanted to stay with their mother in Montreal. "They did not want to go back to Texas," Justice Helene Lebel noted in her ruling. The children, then 11 and 9, had spent virtually their entire lives in Montreal. Their mother had returned with them to Canada last January after a four-month attempt at reconciliation with her estranged husband, Predrag Perisic, who had moved to Texas in 2007 seeking work. But Judge Lebel dismissed the children's concerns. She agreed with Mr. Perisic's contention that under international law their "habitual residence" was Texas, where they had lived a total of 137 days, and they should be returned there to let the courts determine their fate.

They were uprooted from school—Danyela's Grade 6 graduation dress went unworn—and sent to live with their father.

"They do not wish to go back so they will certainly be perturbed," Judge Lebel wrote. "However, these children are intelligent and capable of coping. They are not being returned to a place where they will be in danger."

A Dangerous Father

Late Monday afternoon law enforcement officers executing a warrant for Mr. Perisic's arrest arrived at a secluded lake house in Coldspring, Tex., where he was in hiding with his son and daughter. After clearing the ground floor, they had begun moving upstairs when they heard gunshots coming from the back of the house.

Deyan Perisic, 10, was taken by ambulance to hospital, where he was pronounced dead. His sister Danyela, 12, had been shot eight times and was airlifted to a Houston hospital, where her condition is listed as stable. Their father is in custody, charged with murder.

Mary Quinn, the Houston attorney for the children's mother, Vera Vucerakovich, said there were plenty of warning signs that Mr. Perisic was dangerous. "If you talk to my client, she all along has believed that this man was capable of violence," Ms. Quinn said in an interview. "That was part of the reason that they weren't living together."

She said the Superior Court decision sending the children to Texas "was really a horrible ruling. I don't understand why the court that heard that decided that Texas was the habitual residence of these kids when they had grown up in Canada and only lived in Texas for a few months."

Judge Lebel was interpreting the 30-year-old Hague Convention [on the Civil Aspects of International Child Abduction], which deals with international child abduction. Mr. Perisic contended that under the convention, Ms. Vucerakovich had unlawfully removed her children from Texas when she returned to Montreal in January.

Even though she still had a house in Montreal, Judge Lebel agreed that the move to Texas had been for an indefinite period and the state was now the children's place of residence. While there was no evidence Mr. Perisic had been violent toward the children, she acknowledged he was far from perfect. "However, in any event, the case law that has evolved under the Hague Convention is to the effect that, while family violence is a serious matter and may warrant some special precautions, it is not a ground for refusing the return of a child under the law or the convention," she said.

The Legal Battle Moves

After the children's removal from Canada, the legal battle moved to Texas, where District Court in Harris County rejected Justice Lebel's conclusion and sent the matter back to Quebec. On Oct. 26, Quebec Superior Court Justice Marie-Christine Laberge granted Ms. Vucerakovich custody of the children and ordered Mr. Perisic to turn them over to her at her Houston attorney's office.

> ## Custody Battles Put Children at Risk
>
> There are, on average, about 140,000 divorces in Britain each year. That's a lot of unhappiness and a lot of anger. One rough index of that increasing parental strife is our soaring rate of child abductions, up 20 per cent in 2009. At least 500 children a year are kidnapped and taken abroad by an estranged parent....
>
> Revenge killings are almost always carried out by men and are triggered by sexual jealousy. A woman leaves an abusive relationship and the man hits back by destroying her most precious possession—her child.
>
> *Kevin Toolis,*
> *"How Can Any Father Kill His Child?"* Mail Online,
> *January 4, 2010. www.dailymail.co.uk.*

Instead, he pulled the children from school and fled the home he lived in with his twin brother in La Porte, Tex. The brother, Nenad Perisic, told Houston TV station KHOU on Tuesday that his brother "was a man of his word" because he had warned his wife. "He told her a couple of months ago, 'If you don't get together, you know what I'm going to do to the kids. They can go over my dead body to Montreal,'" the brother said.

The Hague Convention leaves no place to examine the children's interests.

On Sunday evening, Zivorad Subotic, the priest at Montreal's Holy Trinity Serbian Orthodox Church, received a call from a distraught Predrag Perisic, who had been a parishioner when he lived in Montreal. He asked the priest to call his wife and tell her he would kill the children and commit suicide if she did not stop the legal proceedings," Mr. Subotic said.

"I told him you don't have the right to kill even yourself, or your kids. But he was very much out of his mind, I think. . . . He was so desperate." He relayed the message to Ms. Vucerakovich and gave her the phone number from which Mr. Perisic had called. He did not call police but was contacted by a Montreal detective on Monday and filed a report.

Jonathan Shulak, Ms. Vucerakovich's lawyer in Montreal, said the Hague Convention leaves no place to examine the children's interests.

"How do you make decisions regarding children without looking at their best interests? How does that make sense to anyone?" he asked. "There is no common sense involved here. We had a judge who was by the book, who had a strict interpretation of the law and applied the law as is. She had room for discretion once the children expressed their opposition, but she didn't feel their testimony should be given great weight."

VIEWPOINT 6

Parricide in the United States

Kathleen M. Heide

In the following interview with CBS News, University of South Florida professor of criminology Kathleen M. Heide discusses cases of family violence in which children kill their parents. She notes that certain factors increase the likelihood of a child killing a parent, but also asserts that parricide is difficult to predict. She divides parricide offenders into three broad categories: severely abused children, dangerously antisocial children, and severely mentally ill children. Parental boundary setting is important, Heide argues, and she also urges parents to seek help when a child displays certain behaviors.

As you read, consider the following questions:

1. What percentage of fathers and mothers who are killed by their offspring are killed by children under eighteen?
2. Heide states that severely abused children who commit parricide typically have a long-standing history of what? For what disorder do these children typically meet the diagnostic criteria?
3. What weapon do most juveniles and adolescents choose to commit parricide?

[CBS News] *What prompted your study of parricide?*

[Kathleen M. Heide] I began evaluating juvenile killers in the early 1980s. Some of these youths had killed their parents.

Kathleen M. Heide, "Q&A: Why Kids Kill Parents," CBS News, April 10, 2010. Copyrigth © 2010 by CBS News. All rights reserved. Reproduced with permission.

Family Violence and Children

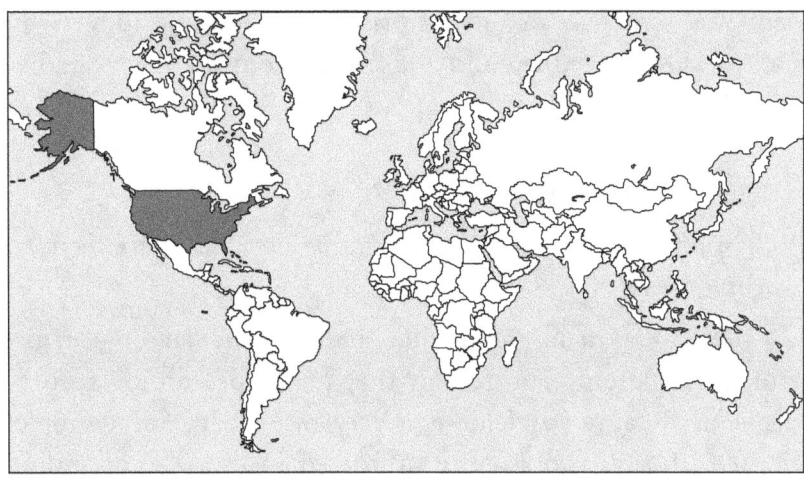

When I heard the stories and investigated the backgrounds of youths who killed their mothers, fathers, or both parents, it was clear that abuse and neglect typically played a role in these killings. The cases of kids who killed parents were very different from adolescents who killed under other circumstances, such as during the commission of a robbery or a burglary. I found cases of young people killing their parents very disturbing and unsettling.

I decided to write my first book, *Why Kids Kill Parents: Child Abuse and Adolescent Homicide*, after receiving a phone call from "a good kid" who killed his mother and father. The record established that both parents were alcoholics and abused him for years. During the phone call, the boy said, "Dr. Heide, someone has to tell the story about kids like me." Three petitions alleging abuse had been filed by the state social services agency in this case prior to the killings. This boy had been removed from the home for a period of time after it was established in court that the parents had physically abused him. The boy was later returned to live with the parents. Nine months after the social services agency ended its supervision, this boy killed his parents. He was in the process of running away when the deadly confrontation happened. This adolescent was sentenced to life in prison by the same judge who had presided over the child abuse proceedings a few years before the killings.

Parricide Is Hard to Predict

Your study says that parricide cannot be predicted—are there no warning signs?

It is not possible to predict that a particular boy or girl will kill a parent. The reason that parricide cannot be predicted is because parricide is a very rare event. For example, in 2008, 14,180 people were murdered in the U.S., according to FBI [Federal Bureau of Investigation] data. Of these, 117 were mothers and 120 were fathers slain by their biological children. These 337 victims represent about 2 percent of all individuals killed during that year.

Most of the offspring who killed their parents were actually adult children, meaning they were over 18 years of age. My analyses of thousands of parricide cases since the mid-1970s has revealed that approximately one out of four fathers (25 percent) and one out of six mothers (16 percent) who are killed by their offspring are killed by children under 18. If the age of the child is extended to include 18- and 19-year-olds, the percentages of fathers killed by children under age 20 increases to 33 percent of fathers and 25 percent of mothers.

> *In 2008, 14,180 people were murdered in the U.S. . . . 117 were mothers and 120 were fathers slain by their biological children.*

In addition to the small number of cases of parricides in relation to all homicides, studies have shown that it is hard to predict violent behavior, unless there is a history of violent behavior by a particular individual.

Although it is not possible to predict that a youth will kill his or her parent, research has indicated there are certain factors, if present, that increase the likelihood of a youth killing a parent. These include:

- The youth is raised in a chemically dependent or other dysfunctional family.
- An ongoing pattern of family violence exists in the home.
- Conditions in the home worsen, and violence escalates.
- The youth becomes increasingly vulnerable to stressors in the home environment.
- A firearm is readily available in the home environment.

When these conditions are present, parents or other adults need to take action to get help. When I see families in these situations, one of the first things I ask is whether there is a firearm in the home. If so, I advise the parents to remove the gun from the home until conditions improve substantially. My research and studies by others show that in the majority of cases, children and adolescents use guns to kill both fathers and mothers. My analyses of thousands of cases show that youths under 18 are significantly more likely to use firearms to kill their parents than adult offenders.

Is there an age when a child is more likely to kill their parent (juvenile versus adult)? And is there an overwhelming motivation?

There is no specific age. However, age is indeed relevant when looking at likely motivations or factors contributing to the homicide. Motivations for the killing are very important, as they are related to how much risk the parricide offender is to society and what should be done in terms of justice. Children and adolescents are most likely to kill to end abuse or to get their own way. Sometimes they kill because of severe mental illness. However, severe mental illness is not as much of a factor with young parricide offenders as with older parricide offenders.

Adults who kill their parents, particularly those who are middle-aged, are likely to kill their aging parents because of severe mental illness, such as psychosis or severe depression. They also kill for antisocial reasons, such as to get their parents' assets. Abuse alone is rarely the driving force for an older adult to kill a parent because a healthy adult has options a child under 18 does not have. A healthy adult, for example, can leave the home of the aging parent or cut ties with an abusive parent. When conditions warrant it, such as the deteriorating health of an aging parent, perhaps, complicated with substance abuse, a healthy adult can take action to have the parent hospitalized or put in a nursing facility.

The Three Categories of Parricide

In your book and in your recent article, "Matricide: A Critique of the Literature," you profile three distinct categories of parricide offenders—can you detail them for us?

From my review of others' reports and my own clinical evaluations, I have found that most cases can be categorized into three primary types of parricide offenders: the *severely abused child*, the *dangerously antisocial child*, and the *severely mentally ill child*. Among children, adolescents, and young adults, the severely abused child and the dangerously antisocial child are most common. Among older adults, the severely mentally ill and the dangerously antisocial types predominate.

Severely abused children (SAC) kill their abusive parent to end the abuse. These individuals have been abused by their parent(s) for years. The abuse is typically known to others. SAC have sought help from others and, yet, the abuse has continued. They often have tried to run away, considered suicide, and, in some cases, have attempted to kill themselves.

Family Violence and Children

Over time, the violence in the home escalates and these individuals become increasingly stressed. They kill the abusive parent because they are terrified that they or other family members will be seriously harmed or killed. They are typically desperate and see no other way out but murder. These individuals typically have a long-standing history of depression and meet the diagnostic criteria for post-traumatic stress disorder (PTSD).

Dangerously antisocial children (DAC) kill the parent to further their own goals. In these cases, the parent is an obstacle in their path to getting what they want. These individuals, for example, may kill to have more freedom, to continue dating a person to whom the parents object, and to inherit money they believe is eventually coming to them. DAC have a pattern of violating the rights of others when it suits them. Typically this behavioral pattern begins in childhood. Youths who continuously defy adults, do what they want on their own time frame, and do not accept responsibility for their actions over a significant period of time will likely be diagnosed as having oppositional defiant disorder. If this behavioral pattern is not corrected, the youth often will engage in criminal activities that may include violence towards people or animals, destruction of property, deceitfulness or theft, and/or serious violations of rules by parents, such as staying out all night or being truant from school. At this point, the youth will likely be diagnosed as having a conduct disorder. If this pattern of violating the rights of others continues past age 18, it is likely that this individual may be diagnosed as having an antisocial personality disorder. This type of parricide offender is far more dangerous to society than the first in terms of re-offending and hurting other people in the future.

Severely mentally ill children (SMIC) kill the parent largely as a result of severe mental illness. Diagnoses commonly made include psychosis and severe depression. A long-standing history of mental illness is generally easy to document in these cases. SMIC are typically on psychotropic medication and are most apt to kill when they stop taking it. They may kill the parent, for example, because they have delusions (bizarre and irrational beliefs) that the parent is the devil. They may report hearing God's voice commanding them (a hallucination—false sensory experience) to kill the parent.

Dangerously antisocial children ... kill the parent to further their own goals. In these cases, the parent is an obstacle in their path to getting what they want.

How do you determine the type of parricide offender? Is it as straightforward as it seems?

Determining the type of parricide offender is not as easy as it may seem. An accurate assessment takes time and serious study. The adage "You can't judge a book by its cover" often applies here. For example, in parricide cases involving young offenders, severe mental illness is typically ruled out. In many cases, the question becomes, is the boy or girl a severely abused or dangerously antisocial child? On the one hand, I have had several cases of youths who initially appeared dangerously antisocial, but careful evaluation revealed otherwise. Some youths who have been severely abused may adopt a tough exterior that suggests to others that they may be antisocial when they are not. On the other hand, I have encountered youths where extensive abuse was evident and who were extremely dangerous. Even when abuse is present, the critical question remains: What propelled the youth to kill the parent?

Making this judgment requires an in-depth evaluation by a mental health professional who is knowledgeable about family violence. In my practice, I focus on juveniles, adolescents, and young adults who kill parents. In my cases, I spend hours evaluating the parricide offender and routinely consult with surviving family members. I also speak with the offender's friends and teachers when possible. Family members are essential in corroborating abuse, the early history of the child, and family dynamics. Friends and teachers can provide important information about what the youth is like, how the youth handles stress, and what changes occurred in the youth's behavior over time. I review police reports, depositions of witnesses, school and medical records, and social services records if they exist with respect to dependency and delinquency histories. I routinely consult with other mental health professionals who may have had earlier contact with the child.

Boundary Setting

Can you talk about the importance of boundary setting and parental respect for children in regards to their parents?

Setting boundaries is very important in raising children. Good parenting requires setting limits and disciplining children when they do not abide by them. From the time they are toddlers, children test limits and challenge parents. For example, a 3-year-old wants an ice cream sandwich right before dinner. The mother says no, explaining that they will be eating dinner soon. The child screams, cries, and kicks his feet in protest. If the mother, exhausted from a long day, gives in, thinking it is not worth the hassle, the child has learned an important lesson. The child can wear his mother out and get what he wants by temper tantrums and bad behavior. Unless the mother changes that behavior, the child will continue to challenge her and his bad behavior will escalate.

In parricide cases, I have seen good parents overindulge their children with fatal results. These parents often love their children very much and do not want to fight with them over "little things." These parents reason that these challenges— staying up late, getting another toy at the store—are not really important. The problem is that over time the "little things" become bigger and bigger issues. At 15, 16, or 17 years of age, the son or daughter is now saying, "I am going out, I am taking the car, I am dating who I want." The parent appropriately

Family Violence

Deadly Statistics

- On average, about five parents are killed by their biological children in the United States every week.

- Of the approximately 250 parents killed by their offspring each year, about 100 of these victims are mothers. Despite the frequency, little is known about the perpetrators, particularly when they are females.

- Most mothers who are slain by their offspring are killed by sons. However, the involvement of daughters in matricides is still quite substantial. From 1976 to 1999, the killers in approximately 1 of 6 matricides were daughters.

- Most matricides involve adult offenders. The number of offenders younger than 18 arrested for killing their mothers in the 24-year study period mentioned above ranged from 8 to 24 per year and averaged 17 per year. Girls younger than 18 were the killers in 20 percent of the matricide incidents committed by juveniles.

- The number of mothers killed by daughters under 18 ranged from 1 to 7 per year, and averaged less than 4 per year.

- Analyses since the mid-1970s to now provide no evidence that the incidence of parricide is increasing. Available data suggest, in contrast, that the killings of parents have decreased over the last 30 years.

CBS News,
"Q&A: Why Kids Kill Parents,"
April 10, 2010. www.cbsnews.com.

steps in and says "no." However, the adolescent has not learned to respect the parent and to accept the parent's authority. The youth has not learned that you do not always get your way. The youth has no frustration tolerance, meaning that he does not know how to deal with disappointment, and gets angry. Sometimes the anger is so intense that it erupts into deadly rage.

Is matricide more prevalent in single-parent families?

That question is a hard one to answer because there are no national data that record family composition of matricide victims. I have had cases of adolescents who have killed mothers that came from both two-parent and one-parent families. Case reports from other clinicians and researchers also are mixed with respect to family composition when it comes to adolescents who kill mothers.

Based on my cases and other clinical reports in the professional literature, I would hypothesize that female adolescents are more likely to kill mothers when they are in single-family situations because of the added stress that their mothers may be experiencing in these circumstances. These mothers often have the responsibility of supporting themselves and their children without significant financial and emotional support. Overtaxed, they may expect their daughters to take on more responsibilities that would normally be shouldered by a spouse or significant other. The mothers in this situation may be perceived by their daughters as demanding and critical, rather than as appreciative and loving toward their daughters.

Based on my cases and others reported in the professional literature, I would suspect that boys who kill their mothers are more likely to come from two-parent homes where the mother is perceived by the son and possibly the father as controlling or domineering. In the latter case, the mother's behavior is likely to be psychologically abusive to both her son and her husband. Clearly more research is needed to better understand this important area.

With respect to adult matricide offenders, the picture is clearer than with younger offenders. Adult sons and daughters who kill their mothers are much more likely to be living alone with them than with both parents.

Weapons of Choice

What conclusions can you draw from children who choose knives over firearms?

Most juveniles and adolescents who kill parents use firearms as their weapons of destruction. In matricide cases, firearms are the weapon of first choice followed by knives. Interestingly, my analyses of over 1,400 cases of parents killed by juveniles under 18 over the 32-year period 1976–2007, revealed that the percentages of daughters and sons who used knives to kill mothers was the same—23 percent. Thus, about one in four juvenile matricide offenders stabbed their mothers to death.

Adolescents who kill parents often act impulsively. Those who select knives are even more likely to act due to strong feelings rather than to conscientiously plan the killing. Knives are readily available in homes. Grabbing a knife and wielding it requires little planning.

What does it mean when a victim is stabbed multiple times?

Adolescents who kill parents often act impulsively. Those who select knives are even more likely to act due to strong feelings.

It is often indicative of the release of very strong negative emotion. Studies in rats have demonstrated that a positive feedback loop exists between the aggression center in the brain and the release of stress hormones by the adrenal cortex. This feedback loop amplifies aggressive behavior. In essence, stress and aggression form a rapid positive feedback loop. When stress increases, aggression increases. Conversely, aggressive behavior leads to the release of stress hormones.

This mechanism may help to explain how stressors rapidly generate and exacerbate violent behavior. I have had several cases where homicide offenders have repeatedly stabbed their victims. Once in this positive feedback loop, the offender continues to act out violently until his or her rage has dissipated. At this point, the offender is completely exhausted. Often offenders in this situation report later that they are stunned by what they did. It is almost as though they were on "automatic pilot" and suddenly woke up to see the violence that they had inflicted. The prosecution may suggest that, in the case of a victim who has been stabbed 30 times, the offender made 30 conscious decisions as he or she inflicted each wound. Advances in biological research suggest quite the opposite. Once the offender began the assault, his or her ability to stop, think, and conscientiously make choices was severely compromised.

It is normal for teens to test boundaries—when are the clues that adolescent behavior has gone from normal to something more dangerous?

It is indeed normal for teens to test boundaries. They are yearning for independence and trying to establish their own identity and move towards adulthood. Parents should be concerned when youths are engaging in behavior that is reckless and unhealthy, such as drinking, taking drugs, participating in unprotected or indiscriminate sex, staying out late, skipping school, or being involved in a gang activity or delinquent acts. Parents need to make explicit what behavior is acceptable and what behavior is not.

When is it time for parents to seek out professional help?

It is normal for teens to be upset and to sulk when they do not get their own way. However, if the youth withdraws, becomes noncommunicative or belligerent, it is time to get help. Parents should reassure their children that they love them and that they care enough about them to get a third party involved to help the family work through the conflict. Youths will often accept going to a mental health professional if the whole family participates in the therapy. It is important for parents to communicate with their children, to listen, and to be the parents. In some of the parricide cases I have had, parents tried to be their children's friends. Children need their parents to be adults and not try to act as one of their peers. Kids may openly buck the structure. Inwardly, they need, and often crave, stability and reassurance that their parents have the strength to remain in charge.

Periodical and Internet Sources Bibliography

The following articles have been selected to supplement the diverse views presented in this chapter.

Scott E. Carrell and Mark L. Hoekstra	"Domino Effect: Domestic Violence Harms Everyone's Kids," *Education Next*, vol. 9, no. 3, Summer 2009, pp. 58–63.
Cheryl Critchley	"Smacking Is Distinct from Child Abuse," *Herald Sun* (Australia), October 16, 2009, p. 47.
Julie Griffiths	"Murder in the Family," *Community Care*, January 13, 2011, pp. 16–17.
Keiko Hamana and Nobuteru Sakuda	"The Tragedy of Preventable Child Abuse," *Daily Yomiuri* (Tokyo), March 8, 2010, p. 3.
Rozz Lewis	"Think Tank: We Need an Update on Kids' Safety," *Sunday Times*, November 21, 2010, p. 17.
Rosanna Martinello	"Child Abuse, Neglect Has No Place in 21st Century Australia," *Canberra Times* (Australia), September 5, 2010, p. 27.
Claire Miller	"Rise in Child Attacks by Family Members," *South Wales Echo*, April 25, 2011. www.walesonline.co.uk.
Isaac Pinielo	"Parental Child Abuse a Silent Crime," *The Monitor* (Botswana), vol. 27, no. 15, February 1, 2010. www.mmegi.bw.
Bernadette Sesay	"Let's Make FGM a Part of History," *Gender Links* (Johannesburg), March 15, 2011. www.genderlinks.org.za.
Daniel B. Wood	"Sean Goldman Case Highlights Rising International Child Abduction," *Christian Science Monitor*, December 23, 2009. www.csmonitor.com.

CHAPTER 4

Family Violence and Elders

VIEWPOINT 1

Elders Must Seek Help When Abused

Weill Cornell Medical College

In the following viewpoint, the writers offer the facts about the abuse of older family members. Mistreatment of elders can range from physical abuse to emotional, financial, or sexual abuse. Older family members can also be neglected. Older people often react to abuse by blaming themselves, keeping quiet, or believing no one can help them. The writers give advice to older people who think they are being abused, including how to get and accept help. The Weill Cornell Medical College is a medical school associated with New York-Presbyterian Hospital.

As you read, consider the following questions:

1. What family member is most likely to abuse an elderly family member, and under what circumstances?
2. What is the definition of neglect, according to the viewpoint?
3. What might a professional like a physician, social worker, or police officer be required to do if an elderly person talks to them about abuse?

For many older persons, family represents comfort and belonging, and home is typically considered a safe environment. However, 25 years ago this country finally recognized a

Weill Cornell Medical College, "Elder Abuse: When a Family Member Causes Harm," 2006. Copyright © 2006 by New York Presbyterian Hospital. All rights reserved. Reproduced by permission.

national hidden problem called "elder abuse and neglect." The term *elder abuse and neglect,* or *elder mistreatment,* usually implies that a family member is doing something hurtful to an older relative—physically, emotionally, or financially. These hurtful actions might occur only once, periodically, or frequently. They can be done purposefully or accidentally and can result in mild, moderate, or severe pain or suffering. They usually occur in the older person's own home. If this unacceptable behavior is happening to you, you are not alone—these hurtful things are happening to over 1 million older Americans each year. Help is available.

Who Is Likely to Be Hurt by a Family Member?

Anyone age 60 or older might be a victim of elder abuse. Victims are men and women from all ethnic backgrounds and financial situations (rich, middle class, and poor). They can be healthy or sick, with or without memory problems. The person sitting next to you in the doctor's office, on the bus, or at a religious service could be an elder abuse victim. This person could be you.

Who Hurts Older Relatives?

Any family member could be abusive or neglectful, but the most likely to act this way are adult children. They are likely to live with the parent they are abusing and to be financially and emotionally dependent on the parent, making for a strained and difficult—and, at times, dangerous—relationship. Other abusive family members may be spouses, adult grandchildren, or other relatives, such as nieces, nephews, cousins, stepchildren or step-grandchildren, or siblings. It is not unusual to still love the family member who is being hurtful.

What Are Some Examples of Elder Abuse and Neglect?

Every situation is unique. Examples of types of mistreatment are:

1. Mrs. Rose's 37-year-old son, Derek, who has a drug problem, pulled a fistful of his mother's hair out of her head during an argument when she refused to give him money.

Physical Abuse is any behavior that results (or is likely to result) in injuries to the body, such as bruises, cuts, or broken bones. Examples include hitting, pushing, beating or forcibly restraining. These behaviors also instill great fear in the person being hurt.

2. Mr. Koff's 44-year-old, mentally ill daughter, Karen, threatened to rip the phone out of the wall and nail his bedroom door shut while he sleeps if her father didn't let her boyfriend spend the night.

Psychological/Emotional Abuse is any verbal or nonverbal behavior that causes fear, mental anguish, or emotional pain. Examples include name-calling, "the silent treatment," insults, threats, isolating the individual or treating him/her like a child, and controlling behavior.

3. Mrs. Goffard's 21-year-old granddaughter, Ivy, sold her grandmother's jewelry without permission and used the money to pay back a debt to her friend.

Financial Abuse/Exploitation is any behavior that causes you harm through the illegal or improper use of your funds, property, or assets. Examples include coercing the change of a will, bank account, or property transfer, using cash or credit cards without permission or knowledge, or forging signatures on checks.

4. Mrs. Noonan's 32-year-old stepson forced her to watch pornography with him and exposed himself.

Sexual Abuse is any behavior that hurts you sexually or includes unwanted sexual content without your consent. Examples include inappropriate touching, fondling, or kissing, rape, taking photographs in sexually explicit ways, or exposing you to explicit sexual content without your approval.

Family Violence

5. Mr. Simon is cared for by his overwhelmed 51-year-old daughter, Tasha, who often yells at him. She blames her father for ruining her life and is frequently too busy or "forgets" to give her father dinner.

Neglect is when a caregiver fails to provide basic care needs, resulting in bedsores, dehydration, poor hygiene, or poor nutritional status. Examples include withholding food, water, clothing, medication, or help with personal hygiene, or abandonment.

How Does an Older Person React When Abuse Happens?

Feeling guilty, anxious, confused, ashamed, or fearful is a very common reaction to abuse or neglect. You may also become depressed because you see yourself and/or your situation as hopeless and you may begin to avoid others. Many older people do not speak up about what is going on in their own home, which can lead to even more abuse. Sometimes they suffer the pain in silence because of such mistaken beliefs as:

- *"Family matters are private and should stay that way."* If you believe this, then you are less likely to seek help. But without help, chances are that the abuse and/or neglect will worsen.

- *"I have no one to turn to who can help."* It is easy to believe that nobody is available to help, especially since your relative may be isolating you from others. But there are people who will care about you and help you—perhaps a neighbor, friend, doctor, nurse, clergy member—if you can find a way to let them know you are unhappy at home.

- *"The abuse is my fault."* The natural inclination is to blame oneself for the abuse or neglect in order to feel more in control of a situation that is out of your control. Also, part of the self-blame may come from feeling guilty, often a common reaction to being mistreated. You may believe that you did something wrong and therefore you somehow caused the abuse. But no matter what happened in the past—even if you made mistakes you deeply regret—it is never okay for someone to hurt you.

- *"The consequences of speaking up are worse than keeping quiet."* You may be concerned that if you tell an outsider about your situation, you will have to move from your home or, perhaps, live alone. Or you may become confused about the appropriate action to take because of the impact on your family if you report it to the authorities. Speaking up does not automatically mean strangers will control your life. It does increase the likelihood that you will find someone who can help you problem-solve workable alternatives.

- *"I'm so ashamed and embarrassed that my own family member could be behaving in an abusive or neglectful way."* Older people often are ashamed about the mistreatment they are experiencing, so they avoid telling anyone about it. Feeling ashamed usually comes from a fear that others will judge you or your family member harshly if they knew what was happening, and believing their criticism would be too difficult to tolerate. But there are many people who would want to help you and who would not judge you or your relative(s). You just need to ignore those people who do not understand and keep speaking up until you find those who do.

- *"I'm afraid if I break the 'family secret,' the person hurting me will get back at me in a way worse than what is happening now."* Being afraid that the abuser will retaliate is a real concern. However, doing nothing will rarely end an abusive situation; in fact, it usually gets worse. When seeking help, be sure to discuss your very real safety concerns so that a safety plan can be developed to fit your particular circumstances.

Feeling guilty, anxious, confused, ashamed, or fearful is a very common reaction to abuse or neglect.

How Do I Tell if I Am Being Abused or Neglected?

When in a difficult family situation, it can be hard to recognize the signs of abuse or neglect. In general, if you're feeling as if you have a secret "too big" to talk about, feeling guarded or scared when someone asks about your well-being, or feeling like you're hiding something—you need to ask yourself why you desperately don't want others to know or see something going on in your life.

Another sign might be your relative becomes angry with you if you talk to others (especially about family problems). Be concerned if your relative does not "allow" you to go out, have people over, talk freely with others in person or on the phone, meet privately with your physician, or read your own mail. Also, if you are doing things like hiding bruises or injuries, doctor hopping or avoiding visits with family or friends, this could signify that something is quite wrong.

If any of these things are going on for you, allow yourself to consider the possibility of abuse or neglect, and seek help.

What Should I Do if a Family Member Is Hurting Me?

Many communities have victim assistance programs that offer hotlines, counseling, and support groups. Counselors can provide different kinds of help, depending on what you want and need. They can provide emotional support and practical advice, create a plan for safety, and link you to other resources.

Other community programs you might need, depending on your situation, can include legal advice, telephone reassurance calls, safe housing, court protection, money managers, and/or respite programs. If you are being hurt by a family member:

- *Remember that safety is a priority.* Call 911 for help as soon as you feel intimidated and before the situation at home becomes too dangerous or unmanageable. Often people do not think their situation constitutes an emergency until it is too late to get to the phone.

- *Remind yourself over and over that you deserve to live in an environment free of fear and pain.* This may be hard to believe, especially if a loved one has been putting you down. It is important to counteract these messages by telling yourself repeatedly that you have the right to live free from harm.

- *Talk to someone.* Perhaps start by talking with a trusted friend or a family member not hurting you. Remember: If you choose to talk with a professional (like a physician, nurse, social worker, mental health worker, or the police), they may be required by state law to report your situation to Adult Protective Services. (Laws differ from state to state.) If you are uncomfortable with this possibility, before you tell a professional anything about your situation, ask, "If an older person wants to tell you something private about a conflict in the family, will you be able to keep the information confidential, or will you have to tell someone else?" If the answer is "I will have to tell someone else," decide if you want to talk about your situation with that person. Sometimes mistreated older people find the best place to start getting help is with a hotline counselor because of the anonymity you will have.

Family Violence

- *Keep talking to people until you get the help you need.* It is likely that the abuse will not only continue, but also will get worse over time if you do not involve others to help you. Sometimes the first person you speak to will not know what to do or say. Try someone else, even though this may not be easy to do.

- *Do not focus on labels.* It may be hard for you to hear a member of your family labeled as an "abuser" or it may be upsetting to hear someone call you a "victim." This is understandable. The most important thing, however, is to focus on getting help for your situation. Worrying about the label can distract you from this goal.

- *Accept help.* Accept this help for yourself. However, you may want to also find help for your family member. You can start to collect names of resources that may be of help to your abusing relative. Seek service information from the people helping you, as well as, advice on how best to get this information to your relative.

VIEWPOINT 2

In India, the Abuse of Older People by Family Members Is Increasing

Mala Kapur Shankardass

In the following viewpoint, Mala Kapur Shankardass argues that elder abuse in India is an underreported and understudied problem. She contends that such abuse is increasing daily and that it happens at all social levels. Aging women, particularly widows, are likely to be abused by family members. Because the population of India is aging, it is important for India to pass laws and make policies that will protect the elderly. Shankardass also believes the public awareness of the problem must be raised. Shankardass is a gerontologist working with the International Network for the Prevention of Elder Abuse.

As you read, consider the following questions:

1. When did gerontological research, especially in the United Kingdom and United States, begin to focus on elder abuse?
2. How many older people are projected to be living in India by 2020?
3. What does Shankardass state is an important intervention strategy for everyone, particularly women, to undertake?

Mala Kapur Shankardass, "No One Cares About Elder Abuse in India," One World South Asia, June 12, 2009. Copyright © 2009 by Women's Feature Service. All rights reserved. Reproduced by permission.

187

Family Violence

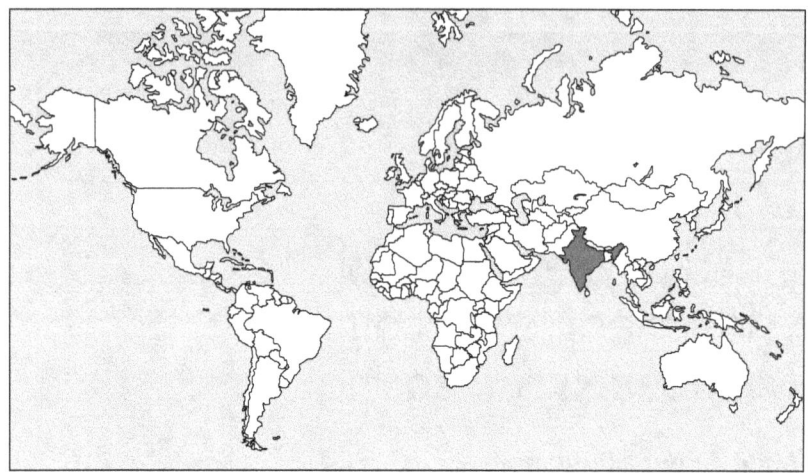

Prema's name translates as "loved one". But in Prema's case, her name is a misnomer. Far from being loved, at her advanced age she finds herself working endlessly for the young woman her husband brought into their home as his new "wife".

Prema, a homemaker who lives near Chandigarh [India], is in her late 60s. She was around 53 when her husband got inclined towards another, younger women. At first, her husband was indifferent towards her, but this has turned to total neglect now.

Her situation is unusual, but it does fall in the category of "elder abuse", a situation in which older people are subjected to abuse and neglect within their families and communities.

An Unaddressed Concern

On June 15 [2009], the world observes [World] Elder Abuse Awareness Day, yet people like Prema continue to suffer neglect and abuse.

It was in the mid-1980s that gerontological research, especially in the UK [United Kingdom] and US [United States], began to focus on elder abuse. But more than three decades later, it remains an unaddressed concern in India, characterised by a lack of conceptual and definitional clarity.

Since this crime is greatly underreported, there is also a conspicuous absence of relevant data on it. The situation is compounded by the fact that not all situations of elder abuse fit neatly into the existing legal categories.

Consequently, elder abuse as a social issue or as one that is relevant to public health figures very inadequately in the public sphere. This has resulted in the underlying causes of abuse—which could in turn have helped in developing appropriate interventions to address it—remaining unidentified.

Already marginalised, the hardships [aging Indian widows] undergo due to age are never adequately realised and their need for more resources to meet their deteriorating health is invariably overlooked.

Elder Abuse Is Increasing

Yet, there is empirical evidence to suggest that in India incidents of abuse and neglect of older people are increasing by the day, both within families and institutions, and that it prevails across classes, castes and religions.

Reports of such abuse have come in from every state in the country and it takes place in both rural and urban settings.

What is a particularly disquieting trend is the vulnerability of aging women to oppression in various forms. Given existing structures of gender discrimination, women run a greater risk than men of becoming victims of material exploitation, financial deprivation, property grabbing, abandonment, verbal humiliation, emotional and psychological torment.

When they fall seriously ill, it is more likely than not that it is the elderly women in the family who will be denied proper health care.

There is also a greater tendency to dismiss the gendered aspects of elder abuse. They rarely come to light.

This is because such attacks are made invisible by the belief that they are "internal" or "domestic" matters that need to be sorted out by the concerned individuals and not one that can be addressed publicly.

There is also a widespread understanding that the neglect, deprivation and marginalisation of older women are the normal consequences of aging.

The most common abuse [elderly Indian] women face is being denied independent social and economic resources.

The Plight of Aging Widows

The plight of young widows has been well-documented and commented upon in the country, but what has been overlooked are the traumas they undergo as a result of aging.

Already marginalised, the hardships they undergo due to age are never adequately realised and their need for more resources to meet their deteriorating health is invariably overlooked.

It is unfortunate that even organisations involved in women's activism have paid insufficient attention to this helpless and hapless section of the population.

In fact, women's organisations have so far tended to focus more on the dilemmas of middle-aged women who have to balance their own personal and career needs with the demands of looking after both the young and older generations within their families.

The research that I have personally conducted as a gerontologist has been revealing. I have come across women who have been hit, or more specifically slapped, by their sons, daughters-in-law, daughters and husbands.

Some older women have told me that they have had things thrown at them when they have not done something according to the desires of family members. They have been pushed around or restrained from doing something they had wanted to do, whether it is cooking, housekeeping, or participating in activities outside the home. Many have reported being spat upon while some have been falsely framed for dowry harassment.

But the most common abuse these women face is being denied independent social and economic resources. Most of them carry on doing the backbreaking domestic chores that they have done all their lives. The luxury of a little leisure, a little care, is something that has always eluded them.

Elder Abuse Is Difficult to Measure

While it is difficult to accurately measure the extent of the problem on a national scale, given the fact that most families deny that such abuse takes place within the four walls of their homes, we do know that the number of older people in our midst is growing.

Current estimates put the 60-plus population at around 90 million and India is projected to have a population of 142 million older people by 2020. Given this demographic reality, what kind of action can the country take at the individual and societal level to alleviate abuse and neglect?

How can we generate thought and action from the health, welfare and criminal justice perspectives, which could contribute to a life free of violence, mistreatment and neglect for our elderly? How can we ensure greater acknowledgement and awareness of the need for older men and women to live a life of dignity and respect?

Law Alone Will Not Solve Elder Abuse

Some argue that a good legal regime will help victims of abuse and neglect among the elderly. India, like many other countries in the world, has adult protection provisions similar

Family Violence

to those in Europe, the UK, Canada, South Africa and USA.

But will an act like the Maintenance and Welfare of Parents and Senior Citizens Act, 2007 prove a deterrent to abuse? The problem here is that senior citizens, especially women, do not actively seek justice on issues like these. There is a need to raise public awareness on the issue and set up fast-track systems that will enable older persons to access justice more easily.

For me, an important intervention strategy is for everyone, particularly women, to start preparing for old age even when they are relatively young. It is essential that each individual understands the legal, social and financial factors that shape their lives throughout their life span, and build the necessary support networks.

This will go a long way in helping them take the necessary practical steps to secure their future and protect their rights, even as they advance in years.

VIEWPOINT 3

In Israel, Family Members Abuse and Neglect the Elderly

Judy Siegel-Itzkovich

In the following viewpoint, Judy Siegel-Itzkovich examines the plight of elderly Israelis who suffer various kinds of abuse at the hands of their children. She summarizes a Hebrew film that illustrates how a situation between a mother and daughter can begin happily but end in neglect and despair. Although the film is fictional, it mirrors many real-life situations. The writer also notes that a series of laws have been passed to protect the elderly. She also lists how someone can recognize the signs of physical abuse. Siegel-Itzkovich is the health and science correspondent for the Jerusalem Post.

As you read, consider the following questions:

1. In what percentage of the cases of elder abuse is sexual abuse a factor, according to the viewpoint?
2. What Israeli law provides funding for at least part-time help for the dependent elderly?

Judy Siegel-Itzkovich, "When Old Age Isn't Golden," *The Jerusalem Post*, February 7, 2010. Copyright © 2010 by *The Jerusalem Post*. All rights reserved. Reproduced with permission.

Family Violence

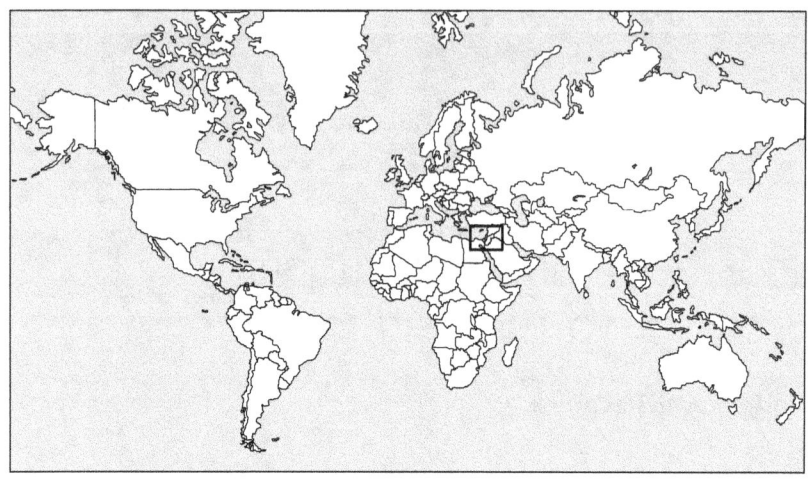

3. What percentage of elderly Israelis responded in a 2005 survey that they had suffered some kind of abuse or neglect?

They spent nights and days caring for their children—feeding, bathing and dressing them, and nursing them back to health when they were ill. They invested a few decades in caring for others. But when elderly Israelis lose their health, strength and/or mental abilities, almost a fifth of them suffer some kind of neglect or abuse at the hands of their children, spouse or other caregiver.

As many societies lose their veneration of the old, elder abuse has begun to creep in, but it was not recognized by the social welfare or law enforcement authorities until recent decades. If a country is judged by the treatment given its weakest elements, surely verbal, physical, social, psychological, financial, criminal and even sexual abuse of the aged is a black mark.

Elder abuse was among the subjects raised at the 10th annual conference of Nefesh Israel, a voluntary organization of observant social workers, psychologists, psychiatrists and others headed by Dr. Judith Guedalia and Leah Rosen. The conference was held recently at the Jerusalem Michlalah.

Forms of Elder Abuse

Sarah Halperin, a Jerusalem municipality social worker who focuses on the treatment, intervention and prevention of elder abuse, said that from her experience, many old people talk about their fears of being preyed upon when they go to cash their National Insurance Institute old-age pension, worried that someone will pounce on them to take it. She added that there are cases of bank accounts and other property being taken over by relatives. Grown children may threaten to disconnect their parents from beloved grandchildren unless they sign over property. They may denigrate them by saying they have "one foot in the grave" or treating the old person like a child and calling him or her "sweetie."

When elderly Israelis lose their health, strength, and/or mental abilities, almost a fifth of them suffer some kind of neglect or abuse at the hands of their children, spouse, or caregiver.

A husband may isolate his less-powerful spouse, preventing her from going to the golden-age club, for example or cutting her off from safe surroundings, making her more dependent; or it could be a woman abusing her weak husband. Physical violence is less common, as is sexual abuse, which reportedly occurs in about three percent of the cases, but "we think it is underreported because of shame. It is hard for people to talk about."

The young social worker recalled that she led a support group for elderly religious women, and was finally told by four of the 12 that they suffered sexual abuse by their husbands, one a man in his late 80s. But she added that it goes both ways; she knew of an elderly man who sexually abused his foreign caregiver.

Family Violence

The Story of an Aging Woman

"Elder abuse occurs in every community and culture. It can be active or passive neglect, such as making sure the refrigerator is almost empty," said Halperin. She presented a heartrending, 30-minute, Hebrew film made by Yohanan Veller about a serious but fictional case of elder abuse that begins happily. A widow lives alone in her apartment, is physically and socially active, friendly with neighbors, able to take care of herself and her devoted dog. She hosts her single daughter for Shabbat meals, is able to shop for food and cook. Her refrigerator is full. Her son, however, almost never comes to visit, as he is always "busy" and full of excuses about having to care for his own family.

But then one horrible day, the heroine of the story falls in the street and breaks her hip. Her daughter volunteers to live with her and help until her pain subsides and she is mobile. But the daughter needs help and direction herself, as she is constantly fired from jobs as a supermarket checkout worker and even cleaning worker because of her lateness and difficulty functioning. The only hopeful moment in her life is when she buys a fruit tart covered with whipped cream in a cheap café and scratches lottery tickets to see if she won; inevitably, her investment in luck fails, and she is left with nothing.

Before the mother is discharged from the hospital, the staff social worker tells the daughter the mother will need help, but she never sends a professional to the home to find out how the patient is managing or if the daughter is capable of taking care of her. The mother's recuperation stalls, and she is shown moaning in bed.

A Neglectful Daughter

Her daughter, again dismissed from her job, becomes increasingly dysfunctional. She gets fed up with having to take the dog out twice a day for a walk, leading to her abandoning the animal in the street and claiming it "ran away." Her mother is devastated, begging her to search for it with a friendly next-door neighbor, but to no avail. The happy scenes of Shabbat dinners are replaced by meager pickings, and even lightbulbs stop working, so they nibble their food in half darkness.

When the neighbor realizes that the daughter is keeping the mother isolated, she calls the social welfare authorities, but a social worker is shooed away by the daughter and not allowed into the apartment. The daughter then attempts to clean the floor, which is covered with dirty dishes, dirty clothes and animal excrement, but when the social worker returns, she sees clear signs of neglect.

However, when the mother is gently questioned, she praises her daughter for her "devotion," and pooh-poohs any mention of the abysmal conditions in the apartment. The social worker consults with her superiors, but nothing comes of it.

Then the next-door neighbor again calls the authorities after hearing moans from the apartment. No one opens the door, so they climb in through the balcony. The poor woman is found puffy-faced, helpless, in serious condition and alone, having fallen on the floor. In the hospital, the doctor comes out to the weeping daughter and tells her that although he struggled to save her, she has died.

But that is not the end. The maker of the film presents a "what if" alternate ending that shows the mother being told by a social worker that she could thrive in a home for the elderly. She is shown happy and thriving among people her age. If somebody in the fictional story had pointed her in the right direction after her injury, there could indeed have been a happy ending.

Halperin queries the participants in her workshop at the conference to suggest how the scenario went wrong. "The system failed her," they responded unanimously. A woman in the audience with professional experience in the field noted that the picture portrayed in the film was even too pretty, as the

> ## Israeli Elderly Fail to Report Abuse
>
> According to an article in the August 2007 issue of the *Journal of the American Geriatrics Society*, researchers discovered the following in a study of 730 persons aged 70 and older at the Rambam and Hadassah medical centers:
>
> - 5.9% of the respondents stated that they had experienced abuse;
>
> - 21.4% were identified as having evident signs of abuse as assessed by trained interviewers; and
>
> - More than 70% of those who stated they had been abused had evident signs of abuse, and were considered by the researchers to be at high risk for further abuse.
>
> *Compiled by editor.*

average Israeli municipal social worker has so many clients that only if one is in major danger will she deal with it.

Halperin said she is currently dealing with an elderly woman suffering from Alzheimer's disease whose "caregiver" is a 35-year-old daughter who lives with her. Not far from the story in the movie, the daughter has borderline psychological problems and neglects her.

"We saw to it that the daughter is getting psychiatric help. After working with the two of them for 18 months, the old woman agreed to have a professional caregiver come in and live with her. Now the daughter is married and has a child.

"That is our direction toward rehabilitation. One can't call the police in all the time and punish the daughter. We try to intervene to help both the parent and the adult child."

Laws Help Prevent Abuse

Women live longer than men, said Halperin, so they are usually dependent, have lower status and are at higher risk for abuse. Living with an adult child can be a bonus, but it can also be very bad. The adult child must be helped to ease the burden. The geriatric nursing law provides funding for at least part-time help for the dependent elderly....

[Dr. Sara] Alon notes that since 1989, a series of laws has been passed aimed at protecting the elderly from abuse; professionals in the field are required to know their details so they can intervene more effectively. A 2005 Israeli national survey of a representative sample of old people living alone showed that 18.4% admitted suffering some kind of abuse or neglect during the previous year. "Although the extent of the problem is worrisome," she writes, "we witness difficulties in exposing it."

Women live longer than men ... so they are usually dependent, have lower status and are at higher risk for abuse.

She defines the result of elder abuse and neglect as "a change in the old person's lifestyle, suffering, harm, an increase in the risk for harm to his well-being, health and safety, and sometimes even to his life." According to the survey, a spouse is the most likely caregiver to commit physical and sexual abuse and limit the victim's freedom; an adult child or other family member is most often a verbal abuser and the one to commit financial abuse.

The negative images of the elderly in Israeli society, the fact that many are hidden from view, and the notion that behavior inside the home need not be made public contribute to difficulties in exposing abuse. The victim is often unaware of his or her rights, ashamed of being maltreated and of "poorly educating" an abusive child, fears being harmed and is dependent on the caregiver.

Social workers and other professionals often fail to act because they are unaware of the phenomenon; unable to identify the signs; concerned that uncovering the crime will cause even more serious problems; fears the abuser; feels helpless; or is overwhelmed by the caseload.

Signs of Abuse

The signs of physical abuse include skin hemorrhages on the face, back, chest, backside and inside parts of the limbs; bite marks; scratches; broken teeth; rubbing of the skin; unexplained fractures and falls; bald patches from hair being pulled, unexplained burns (including by cigarettes); and damage to the genitals. An elderly person who has been abused may be reluctant to look into your eyes, switch physicians frequently, delay going for medical help or refuse to give information, Alon notes. A visit to the person's home may expose many internal door locks or damage to furniture, especially the elderly person's bed. Physical neglect can be identified by undernourishment, filthy, unsuitable clothing and lack of changes of clothing, hypothermia, lack of medication or overmedication, lack of expression on the face and apathy.

VIEWPOINT 4

In Malaysia, Elder Abuse Must Be Reported and Prevented

Esther G. Ebenezer

In the following viewpoint, Esther G. Ebenezer describes the plight of Malaysia's elderly population, arguing that abuse in this group is largely undetected. She defines many categories of abuse, including physical, psychological, financial, and neglect. The signs of elder abuse are often mistaken for normal aging, so it is important for health care workers to recognize and report cases of suspected abuse. Educating and supporting caregivers is an important first step. She also asserts that Malaysia should pass an "elder protective act" to help prevent elder abuse. Ebenezer is a psychogeriatrician and a member of the Star Online *health and aging panel.*

As you read, consider the following questions:

1. What is the most common form of elder abuse, according to Ebenezer?
2. Who is most likely to be the abuser of an elderly person?
3. What support groups does Ebenezer mention as being a useful outlet for caregivers caring for disabled elderly?

Elder abuse exists in our society, but it is hardly ever reported. This can cause serious adverse effects on the health and quality of life of the elderly.

Esther G. Ebenezer, "Throw Momma from the Train," *The Star Online*, August 10, 2008. Copyright © 2008 by Esther G. Ebenezer. All rights reserved. Reproduced by permission.

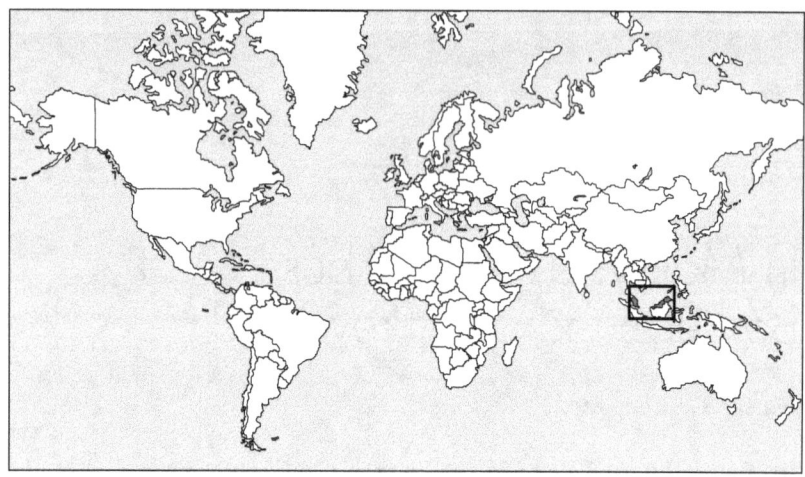

The problem often remains undetected because of poor public awareness and lack of knowledge among health care personnel. We need to be aware of the many faces of elder abuse in our own society—perhaps in the broader context of domestic violence.

Since the Domestic Violence Act 1994 and the Child Act 2001, there has been a wider coverage on this particular legislation in the media. Women and children are more aware of the laws that can protect them, voice their rights and demand justice for them.

On the other hand, although elderly abuse does exist in our society, it remains a subtle and usually untold suffering among older persons. This could be due to lack of awareness in the existence of this phenomenon in our culture. In general the subject of elderly abuse is the least investigated and is given little importance.

Malaysia's Elderly

The segment of elderly population is growing rapidly in Malaysia. Statistics show those 60 years old and above was 6.5% of the population during the year 2000 and is expected to double to 12.2% in the year 2025 because of increasing life expectancy—from 70.8 years to 76.9 years—coupled with reduced fertility rates during the same period.

With advances in medical care and better nutrition, people are living longer. Therefore, the number of dependent elderly with chronic illness is likely to increase. This in turn can pose an increased burden on caregivers such as close family members or nursing home personnel, which could lead to an increased risk of elderly abuse.

> *Statistics [in Malaysia] show those 60 years old and above was 6.5% of the population during the year 2000 and is expected to double to 12.2% in the year 2025.*

There is no formal system of reporting elderly abuse in our society. Hence, proper training programmes and strategies to identify elderly abuse should be implemented in every hospital and at the community level.

This [viewpoint] aims to highlight ways to identify elder abuse and to improve its awareness among Malaysians of all walks of life. It addresses the definition, characteristics of the abused elderly and their abusers as well as strategies to detect and manage the problem.

Definition and Types of Elder Abuse

Elder abuse is a single or repeated act or lack of appropriate action occurring within any relationship where there is an expectation of trust which causes harm or distress to an older person.

Types of elder abuse may be physical, psychological (verbal), financial, sexual or even neglect/abandonment.

Physical abuse is the physical act of violence that commonly includes slapping, hitting, and striking with objects.

Psychological abuse is defined as an act carried out against the elder adult with the intention of causing emotional pain or injury, and it often accompanies physical abuse. Examples of psychological abuse include threats, insults, and statements that humiliate or infantilise the elder.

Exploitation is the most common form of abuse of the elderly, which includes acts of material or financial exploitation. Financial abuse is one of the most difficult types of elder abuse to diagnose as the victim may not be aware of its occurrence or may not know how to seek help.

Some of these include theft of pension checks, threats to enforce the signing or changing of wills or other legal documents, and coercion involving any financial matters. Indicators of potential financial abuse may include unusual bank account activity, sudden change in beneficiaries or agents in a will or advanced directives, or worsening medical conditions due to lack of follow-up or not replenishing drug prescriptions.

Studies suggest that those at risk [of elder abuse] are most likely to be female, widowed, frail, cognitively impaired, and chronically ill.

Exploitation may also occur in the form of fraud schemes; someone may persuade the elderly person to withdraw his/her life savings in a "get rich quick" scheme, or "contractors" convincing the elderly that the house needs repairs, which in reality might be unnecessary.

Neglect of the elderly is also a form of abuse and is often referred to as failure of a caregiver in meeting the needs of the dependent elderly person. This may be intentional or unintentional neglect.

Intentional neglect is to willfully withhold food or medications or medical care. Unintentional neglect could result from ignorance or from genuine inability to provide care. For example, the caregiver may be unable to perform caregiving duties such as bathing or changing an incontinent elderly person. Therefore, an elderly person with poor hygiene, poor nutrition, skin breakdown, and smelling of urine may be neglected either intentionally or unintentionally.

Characteristics of the Abused Elder

It has been established that the problem of abuse and neglect affects all ethnic groups and cuts across all socioeconomic and religious lines. Studies suggest that those at risk are most likely to be female, widowed, frail, cognitively impaired, and chronically ill.

Poor physical health, functional impairment, excessive dependence on the abuser, cognitive impairment and a living arrangement shared with the abuser are some of the risk factors for abuse.

Characteristics of the Abuser

The abuser is most likely the person with whom the elderly person resides. More often, the abuser is a close relative—80% being spouses and children of the victims or a close relative with mental illness or substance abuse problems.

Family members who depend on the elder for financial assistance, housing, or other necessities have a higher risk of becoming abusive. A caregiver's inexperience, a history of family violence, a blaming personality, unrealistic expectations, and economic dependence on the elder often contribute to elderly abuse.

In addition, family characteristics like lack of family support, overcrowding, isolation, marital conflict, and the increased burden of care placed on the caregiver can be a contributing factor.

Detection of Elder Abuse

Signs and symptoms of elder abuse are often confused with normal age-related changes. We are yet to have a health care system in place for such purposes, except medical social workers based in hospitals. Hence the only opportunity for detecting abuse is when the older adult visits a primary care setting or an emergency department.

In order to intervene, one needs to be aware of normal age-related changes as well as the demographic and social backgrounds of the abused and the abuser. Busy clinicians must not merely focus on physical symptoms alone but also on social history from all elderly patients.

Any suspected victim of elder abuse should be interviewed alone to avoid intimidation by the presence of the alleged abuser.

Elderly persons may be hesitant and feel shameful to report that they have been mistreated in front of others. The suspected abuser should be interviewed alone as well.

Unexplained delays in seeking treatment, previous unexplained injuries and the interaction between the patient and the caregiver are important observations.

One should be nonjudgmental, empathetic and understanding of the whole situation. Detailed history should be obtained on caregiving difficulties, family and social support, recent stressors and financial constraints in meeting the needs of the elderly.

Management of Elder Abuse

Whenever mistreatment is confirmed, the highest priority is to ensure the safety of the elderly person. The elderly person who is in immediate danger should be separated from the abuser whenever possible. Hospitalisation can be justified on this basis or by injuries or neglected medical problems so that necessary services can be arranged.

In less urgent cases, the interventions should be tailored to the specific needs of the patient.

Ideally, the management involves a multidisciplinary team consisting of nurses, physicians, social workers and other regulatory bodies. Regular contact between the elderly victim and health care personnel is important to decrease isolation, increase awareness of abuse as well as to monitor the progress in suspected cases of abuse.

Care should be taken to stop the abuse rather than punish the abuser. Health care providers and social workers need to be educated to recognise, treat and be knowledgeable on the social management of an abused elderly.

When a high burden of chronic disease causes stress for the caregiver, a variety of home care or respite services may be required. Unfortunately such services have not developed and are not available for the elderly in our local community.

Disease-specific support groups like the Alzheimer's Disease Foundation Malaysia (ADFM) or Alzheimer's Care Centre (ACC), Stroke Centre can be a useful outlet for caregivers caring for their disabled elderly. Such services should be expanded throughout the country to endow caregivers with health education and coping strategies.

Until today, we do not have any mandatory reporting laws that require practitioners to report suspected elder abuse to an agency. Leaders in health care could make a move to educate the health care providers and the public on elder care.

Last but not least, establishing a legislative "Elder Protective Act" is warranted to protect our vulnerable elderly from untold suffering. They have the right to live with dignity and security. We are committed to developing such services and formulating policies against elder abuse in Malaysia.

VIEWPOINT 5

Some Chinese Senior Citizens in the United States Suffer Elder Abuse

Rong Xiaoqing

The following viewpoint traces the growing problem of elder abuse among the Chinese American community. Because many elderly Chinese Americans do not speak English and rely on their children for financial support, they are both isolated and vulnerable to abuse, asserts Rong Xiaoqing. The writer argues that to help protect elders, social workers and health care personnel must be "culturally competent," understanding that Asian elders are unlikely to accuse their family members of abuse. They must also speak the elder's language. Xiaoqing is a reporter for the Chinese-language newspaper Sing Tao Daily.

As you read, consider the following questions:
1. Why is Jinfu Liu embarrassed, according to the writer?
2. Who sponsors green cards for many Asian seniors?
3. Where was Yuying Sun sent after her husband beat her and his son filed a false police report?

The scourge of family elder abuse affects as many as ... 2 million people in the United States, as well as up to 5 million seniors subjected to financial exploitation.

Rong Xiaoqing, "Cultural Tradition Traps Many Chinese Elder-Abuse Victims in US," *New America Media/Sing Tao Daily*, January 10, 2011. Copyright © 20101 by New America Media. All rights reserved. Reproduced by permission.

Family Violence and Elders

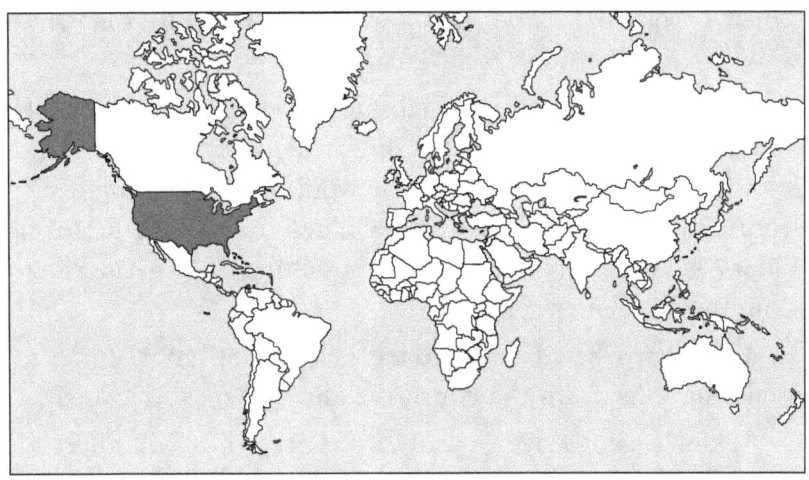

Shame, fear and secrecy surrounding elder abuse have generally made it difficult for experts to obtain exact figures. For Chinese and other Asian American families, the strong influence of traditional culture brings additional challenges to prevention and protection.

"Chinese culture gives higher value to the unity of the family than the individual themselves. It is uncharacteristic for Chinese parents to formally charge their children for abuse," said Xinqi Dong, a researcher at the Rush [University Medical Center] in Chicago.

For this reason, said Dong, "it is more difficult to discover such cases and provide help." These seniors often remain silent about their plight.

One Silent Victim

One of these silent victims is Jinfu Liu, age 75.

Skinny with receding gray hair, the quiet Liu would just look like an ordinary Asian man, except for the scar on his cheek. The scar makes him extremely embarrassed in front of his elderly friends because it was put there by his son's fist.

In the past two years, his son has beat Liu five times. "Once he punched me, and I fell on the floor and fainted.

When I woke up, it took me a long time to figure out why I way lying on the floor," said Liu.

Every time he was attacked, Liu told himself he'd call the police next time. But he never did. If the latest attack had not left him with a bleeding cheek, he would not have sought help from Gin Lee, a specialist at the Chinese Americans Restoring Elders (CARE) Project at the Indochina [Sino-American] Community Center.

However, when Lee suggested helping Liu apply for a restraining order from the court, the abused senior declined.

"I don't want leave my son a bad record. It will affect his future," said Liu. "My son was actually a good boy when he was young. He respected me a lot, and I also secretly favored him over his siblings."

Lee was not surprised. "Many Asian seniors like to keep silent when they are abused by their children. Even when they have to ask for help, they won't like the cops or the court to get involved. No matter how they are treated by their children, they always think for the children," she said.

Elder Abuse Is a Recent Problem in Asia

"Everyone knows revering seniors is a significant part of the Asian culture, so the other side is easily neglected," said Tazuko Shibusawa, an associate professor of social work at New York University, who studies issues affecting Asian seniors.

"In many Asian countries like Japan, people hadn't known the existence of senior abuse until the recent years," Shibusawa went on.

In one study, the Rush [University Medical Center's] Dong found that willful neglect—such as refusing to provide the person food or medicine—is the most common type of abuse among Chinese seniors, followed by emotional abuse and financial abuse. Physical abuse is rare. Although this was a small study, these findings are no different than among whites.

"The more seniors rely on their adult children, the more likely they are to become abuse victims," said Peter Cheng, executive director of Indochina Sino-American Community Center, which operates the only senior protection program in the Chinese community in New York.

> *One study ... found that willful neglect—such as refusing to provide the person food or medicine—is the most common type of abuse among Chinese seniors, followed by emotional abuse and financial abuse.*

Cheng continued, "Many Asian seniors hold green cards sponsored by their children, and they don't speak much English and have few other relatives or friends they can go to. This makes them more vulnerable than seniors in the mainstream community."

Dong noted that in addition to experiencing stress from immigration in later life, filial piety, although highly valued in Asian cultures, can become a fuse for abuse.

"Filial piety requires children to obey the parents and support the parents financially. These are not the obligations of children in the American culture. When the young people cannot meet the expectation of the seniors, it often leads to conflicts," said Dong.

Pauline Yeung[-Ha], an attorney with Grimaldi and Yeung, a New York law firm specializing in aging and disability, said, "In most of our senior abuse cases, the victim is exposed during the dispute among siblings over the assets of the senior's. Few Asian seniors would come to us themselves," said Yeung.

Adult protection specialists in other cities voice the same frustrations. For example, Self-Help for [the] Elderly, a service agency in San Francisco's Chinatown, takes on about three elder abuse cases every month. They refer most cases to the city's Adult Protective Services agency, to which social workers are mandated to report such cases.

> ## More Elder Abuse Is Likely
>
> Reflecting the rapid national growth of Asian elders, the population of seniors 60 or older is 93,000 and will more than double in 10 years.... And the population growth is likely to be accompanied by a rise in abuse cases....
>
> Familial piety is so highly valued in the Asian culture, contributing to the image of Asian Americans as a model minority, that many people, including Asian Americans, don't realize that senior abuse exists in this community.
>
> "The more a culture emphasizes a certain value, the harder for people from this cultural background to openly talk about behaviors that go against the value," said Peter Cheng, executive director of Indochina Sino-American Community Center.
>
> Rong Xiaoqing,
> "Chinese Seniors in U.S. Fall Victim to Elder Abuse (Part I),"
> New America Media, January 6, 2011. http://newamericamedia.org.

"It's very rare to see Asian seniors come to us to make complaints," said Vivien Wong, Self-Help for the Elderly's director of social services.

Protecting Seniors Is a Community Responsibility

Other than the issue of saving face and concerns for their adult children, the silence of Asian victims also stems from their ignorance of the concept of senior abuse. Many times, they don't even realize they've become victims.

Attorney Akiko Takeshita, observed, "When abused, many Asian seniors would think this is their fate, or they'd say, 'My children are rude to me.'"

Takeshita, a lawyer with Asian Pacific Islander Legal Outreach, a legal assistance organization in the San Francisco Bay area, continued, "But if your children take away your jewelry or beat you up, it is not simply 'being rude.'"

Important as it is, raising awareness about elder abuse is not an easy task. Many seniors don't like to attend workshops on elder abuse because it might signal that they are victims—"face losing" in their perspective.

Service providers have to be creative. "When we offer a workshop, we always tell the audience that this may not be for them, but they can help others after they learn more about senior abuse," said Vivien Wong of Self-Help for [the] Elderly.

A culturally competent approach is the key to victim protection. "Many abusers are family members, and the Asians believe what happens in the family stays in the family," Takeshita said. Because victims often don't want to punish their abusers, Takeshita said, service providers also need to work with the adult children, "so when we are out of the picture, they still can live together."

Sometimes, a social worker's understanding of the victim's language and culture can save a life. Ask 67-year-old Yuying Sun. She married a Chinese American and moved to the New York [area] five years ago, but Sun said her husband and his children treated her like a servant.

After her husband beat her, she was sent to a mental health evaluation institute in a hospital in the Bronx, thanks to his son's 911 call and false report to the police.

Sun, who doesn't speak English, was placed in a locked unit with mentally ill patients and no interpreter. Lee, of the Indochina [Sino-American] Community Center, heard about her case through a services organization in the Bronx and went to the hospital to see her.

Sun told her she was thinking of hanging herself. "I thought my life was totally collapsed and could not see any hope. If she hadn't rescued me, I'd have been dead now," said Sun, who has since been fighting in court for her rights.

"We may only be a small program, but we want people in the community to understand, if you and I don't stand up to fight against senior abuse, many lives of the seniors would be withering in silence," said Lee.

Periodical and Internet Sources Bibliography

The following articles have been selected to supplement the diverse views presented in this chapter.

Marie-Therese Connolly	"A Hidden Crime," *Washington Post*, January 27, 2008, p. B01.
Department of Justice Canada	"Abuse of Older Adults: Department of Justice Canada Overview Paper," June 2009. www.justice.gc.ca.
European Association for Injury Prevention and Safety Promotion	"Elder Abuse," *Interpersonal Violence: The Magnitude of the Issue and Measures in Place Within EU-Member States*, 2008. www.eurosafe.eu.com.
Richard Guilliatt	"What's Really Happening Behind These Doors?," *Weekend Australian*, June 30, 2007, p. 28.
Thomas Kim	"Big Jump in Reported Elder Abuse," *Press* (Christchurch, New Zealand), January 28, 2009.
Oliver Mupila	"The Silent Cancer of Elder Abuse," *Times of Zambia*, July 22, 2008. www.times.co.zm.
Brenda Power	"Before You Blame the Carers for Abuse, Blame the Children," *Sunday Times* (London), December 19, 2010, p. 16.
Straits Times (Singapore)	"Parental Abuse: The Family Remains the Front Line," June 30, 2009.
Katherine G. Weiss and Brian Krase	"Older Victims of Violence Face Unique, Daunting Challenges," *Legal Intelligencer*, November 5, 2010. www.law.com.
Hannah Winkler	"Murder Spotlights Domestic Abuse of Elderly," *Times News* (Burlington, NC), July 16, 2006. www.thetimesnews.com.

For Further Discussion

Chapter 1

1. Using the information from the viewpoints in this chapter, who is most likely to suffer from intimate partner violence? To what extent is intimate partner violence a problem for men?

2. Several viewpoints in this chapter argue that intimate partner violence is kept hidden in many countries. What are some reasons people do not report intimate partner and spousal violence? What can be done to draw attention to the extent of the problem? What are some ways women and men could be encouraged to come forward for help?

Chapter 2

1. Several viewpoints in this chapter touch on dowry deaths and bride burnings. What is dowry? How does the practice of dowry lead to family violence? What are nations such as India and Pakistan attempting to do about dowry? How does the custom of dowry devalue women in marriage relationships?

2. What is a so-called "honor killing"? Give some examples found in the viewpoints in this chapter. How can honor killings be differentiated from other forms of domestic violence? How do you think the law should handle honor killing cases? Use information from the viewpoints to support your position.

Chapter 3

1. In many countries of the world, the sex ratio at birth between girls and boys is becoming seriously unbalanced, with the number of boys outnumbering girls to such an

extent that in the future, there will not be enough marriage partners for the boys. Why is this happening, according to the viewpoints in this chapter? What are some of the consequences experts foresee as a result? What can be done to correct the imbalance?

2. Several of the viewpoints in this chapter touch on female genital mutilation. What is this practice? Why is it practiced? Do you think it should be banned everywhere, or do you think that it is an important cultural tradition that people should be able to uphold? Support your answer with evidence from the viewpoints.

Chapter 4

1. Why do elderly people who are being abused by their children or other family members fail to report the abuse? What can be done to protect and help the elderly? What can be done to support family members who provide care for elderly relatives?

2. Why do you think elder abuse is a growing problem in the United States and around the world? What factors are leading to the increase in the number of cases? Predict what you think will happen in the coming years, based on what you know about the demographics of various countries and the information found in the chapter's viewpoints.

Organizations to Contact

The editors have compiled the following list of organizations concerned with the issues debated in this book. The descriptions are derived from materials provided by the organizations. All have publications or information available for interested readers. The list was compiled on the date of publication of the present volume; the information provided here may change. Be aware that many organizations take several weeks or longer to respond to inquiries, so allow as much time as possible.

Africans Unite Against Child Abuse (AFRUCA)
Unit 3D/F Leroy House, 436 Essex Road, London   N1 3QP
 United Kingdom
+44 (0)844 660 8607 • fax: +44 (0)844 660 8661
website: www.afruca.org

Africans Unite Against Child Abuse (AFRUCA) is a London-based organization concerned with cruelty against African children. It raises money to promote the welfare of these children; advocates for changes in policy and legislation to protect children; and provides treatment for abused children. It publishes brochures and articles in both English and French, including "What Is Child Trafficking?," "What Is Child Abuse?," "What Is Witchcraft Abuse?," and "What Is Female Genital Mutilation?"

Asian Task Force Against Domestic Violence
PO Box 120108, Boston, MA   02112
(617) 338-2350 • fax: (617) 338-2354
website: www.atask.org

The mission of the Asian Task Force Against Domestic Violence is to prevent domestic violence among Asian families and provide help for survivors of such violence. The organization maintains a twenty-four-hour multilingual help line;

works to provide shelters for women, children, and other family members at risk of injury from family violence; and raises funds to support this work. It publishes an annual report, monthly e-mail newsletters, and press releases.

Centers for Disease Control and Prevention (CDC)
1600 Clifton Road, Atlanta, GA   30333
(800) 232-4636
e-mail: cdcinfo@cdc.gov
website: www.cdc.gov

The Centers for Disease Control and Prevention (CDC) is the public health arm of the US government. Its mission is to protect health and promote quality of life through the prevention and control of disease, injury, and disability. One important program of the CDC is the Domestic Violence Prevention Enhancement and Leadership Through Alliances (DELTA). Publications include reports, statistics, and fact sheets regarding violence and injury due to family violence.

International Society for Prevention of Child Abuse and Neglect (ISPCAN)
13123 East Sixteenth Avenue B390, Aurora, CO   80045
(303) 864-5220 • fax: (303) 864-5222
e-mail: ispcan@ispcan.org
website: www.ispcan.org

The International Society for Prevention of Child Abuse and Neglect (ISPCAN) is a multinational organization that brings together experts and professionals to work on the prevention and treatment of child abuse and neglect. The organization works toward supporting the United Nations Convention on the Rights of the Child. Publications of the group include the international journal *Child Abuse and Neglect*; nine editions of *World Perspectives on Child Abuse*; a newsletter; and other information regarding the incidence, consequence, and prevention of child abuse and neglect.

National Center on Elder Abuse (NCEA)
c/o Center for Community Research and Service
University of Delaware, 297 Graham Hall, Newark, DE   19716
(302) 831-3525 • fax: (302) 831-4225
e-mail: ncea-info@aoa.hhs.gov
website: www.ncea.aoa.gov

The National Center on Elder Abuse (NCEA) is a national resource center that provides support on behalf of older people and is directed by the US Administration on Aging. The NCEA also provides information and referral to the public. The organization's website includes fact sheets such as "Why Should I Care About Elder Abuse?" and information about ways to prevent and report elder abuse.

National Coalition of Anti-Violence Programs (NCAVP)
240 West Thirty-fifth Street, Suite 200, New York, NY   10001
(212) 714-1184
e-mail: webmaster@avp.org
website: www.avp.org/ncavp.htm

The National Coalition of Anti-Violence Programs (NCAVP) is a coalition of programs that take as their mission the problem of violence committed against and within the lesbian, gay, bisexual, transgender (LGBT), and HIV-affected communities. The organization initiates and supports local anti-violence groups, runs a twenty-four-hour hotline, and serves as a clearinghouse for information. Of special interest is a national report on incidence and circumstances of LGBT domestic violence.

National Committee for the Prevention of Elder Abuse (NCPEA)
1612 K Street NW, Suite 400, Washington, DC   20006
(202) 682-4140 • fax: (202) 223-2099
e-mail: info@preventelderabuse.org
website: www.preventelderabuse.org

The National Committee for the Prevention of Elder Abuse (NCPEA) is an American organization composed of researchers, practitioners, educators, and advocates dedicated to protecting elderly people. The organization publishes the *Journal of Elder Abuse and Neglect* as well as fact sheets and informative articles, all available on its website. Also on the website is an extensive annotated bibliography of resources and journal articles of interest to anyone studying elder abuse.

National Council on Child Abuse & Family Violence (NCCAFV)
1025 Connecticut Avenue NW, Suite 1000
Washington, DC 20036
(202) 429-6695 • fax: (202) 521-3479
e-mail: info@nccafv.org
website: www.nccafv.org

The National Council on Child Abuse & Family Violence (NCCAFV) is a nonprofit organization whose mission is to prevent family violence and child abuse by bringing together community and national stakeholders, professionals, and volunteers. The website provides extensive information concerning child abuse including up-to-date news and fact sheets.

United Nations Information Centres
Public Inquiries Unit, Department of Public Information
United Nations, New York, NY 10017
e-mail: inquiries2@un.org
website: http://unic.un.org

The United Nations Information Centres' website provides full information about the many arms of the United Nations, an organization dedicated to world peace, protection of the world's vulnerable, and protection of the planet. Important and relevant topics found on the United Nations Information Centres' website include reports on the worldwide incidence of family violence; violence against children; and violence against women.

Women Living Under Muslim Laws (WLUML)
International Coordination Office, PO Box 28445
London   N19 5JT
  United Kingdom
e-mail: wluml@wluml.org
website: wluml.org

Women Living Under Muslim Laws (WLUML) is an international organization that provides information and support for women who are governed by laws said to come from Islam, according to the group's website. It focuses on a number of critical issues, the most important of which is violence against women. The organization publishes a journal as well as a newsletter, both of which are available on the website. In addition, WLUML has a plethora of information and downloadable publications available in the Resources section of the website.

World Health Organization (WHO)
Avenue Appia 20, Geneva 27   1211
  Switzerland
+41 22 791 21 11 • fax: +41 22 791 31 11
e-mail: info@who.int
website: www.who.int

The World Health Organization (WHO) is the public health arm of the United Nations. The organization is dedicated to researching, treating, and preventing diseases and educating the world's peoples about their health. The WHO's website offers a global perspective on many of the world's health problems including family violence. Articles, fact sheets, and special reports are available, including those on topics such as violence against women; family and domestic violence; child maltreatment; injuries and violence; and gender inequalities. Also available is a landmark study on domestic violence.

Bibliography of Books

Rogaia Mustafa Abusharaf, ed. — *Female Circumcision: Multicultural Perspectives* (Pennsylvania Studies in Human Rights). Philadelphia: University of Pennsylvania Press, 2006.

Stephen Nmeregni Achilihu — *Do African Children Have Rights?: A Comparative and Legal Analysis of the United Nations Convention on the Rights of the Child.* Boca Raton, FL: Universal Publishers, 2010.

Geraldine Brooks — *Nine Parts of Desire: The Hidden World of Islamic Women.* United Kingdom: Penguin, 2010.

Council of Europe — *Eradicating Violence Against Children.* Brussels: Council of Europe, 2008.

Lina Gonsalves — *Women and Human Rights.* New Delhi, India: APH Publishing, 2008.

Martine Groen and Justine Van Lawick — *Intimate Warfare: Regarding the Fragility of Family Relations.* London: Karnac Books, 2009.

Betsy McAlister Groves — *Children Who See Too Much: Lessons from the Child Witness to Violence Project.* New York: Beacon Press, 2002.

Angela Hattery — *Intimate Partner Violence.* Lanham, MD: Rowman & Littlefield, 2009.

Kate Havelin — *Family Violence: "My Parents Hurt Each Other!"* Mankato, MN: Capstone Press, 2000.

John Hayley, Wendy Stein, and Heath Dingwell	*The Truth About Abuse.* 2nd ed. New York: Facts On File, 2010.
Lee Ann Hoff	*Violence and Abuse Issues: Cross-Cultural Perspectives for Health and Social Services.* Abingdon, Oxon, UK: Routledge, 2009.
Rana Husseini	*Murder in the Name of Honor.* Oxford, UK: Oneworld, 2009.
JoAnn Miller and Dean D. Kundsen	*Family Abuse and Violence: A Social Problems Perspective.* Lanham, MD: AltaMira Press, 2007.
Andrea Parrot and Nina Cummings	*Forsaken Females: The Global Brutalization of Women.* Lanham, MD: Rowman & Littlefield, 2006.
Swati Shirwadkar	*Family Violence in India: Human Rights, Issues, Actions, and International Comparisons.* Jaipur, India: Rawat Publications, 2009.
Rosemarie Skaine	*Female Genital Mutilation: Legal, Cultural, and Medical Issues.* Jefferson, NC: McFarland & Company, 2005.
Souad	*Burned Alive: A Survivor of an "Honor Killing" Speaks Out.* New York: Warnder, 2005.
Randal W. Summers and Allan M. Hoffman, eds.	*Elder Abuse: A Public Health Perspective.* Washington, DC: American Public Health Association, 2006.

Katherine van Wormer and Albert R. Roberts	*Death by Domestic Violence: Preventing the Murders and Murder-Suicides.* Santa Westport, CT: Praeger, 2009.
Unni Wikan	*In Honor of Fadime: Murder and Shame.* Trans. Anna Paterson. Chicago: University of Chicago Press, 2008.
World Health Organization	*A Global Response to Elder Abuse and Neglect: Building Primary Health Care Capacity to Deal with the Problem Worldwide.* Geneva: World Health Organization, 2009.
Robin Wyatt	*Broken Mirrors: The "Dowry Problem" in India.* Thousand Oaks, CA: Sage Publications, 2010.

Index

Geographic headings and page numbers in **boldface** refer to viewpoints about that country or region.

A

Abdel-Qader, Rand, 106, 108
Abduction, child, 160–163
Abdullah II, King, 124
Ableism, 73, 75
Abortion of female children in Asia, 130–137
ACC (Alzheimer's Care Centre, Malaysia), 207
Acceptance of violence
    elder neglect, 190
    intimate partner violence, 28, 49, 53, 76
    See also Cultural pressures
Acid baths, 48, 97
Addiction, 16, 26, 205
ADFM (Alzheimer's Disease Foundation Malaysia), 207
Adolescents. *See* Child abuse; Female genital mutilation; Honor killings; Parricide
Adult protection programs, 211–212
    See also Elder abuse
Adult Protective Services, 211
Afghan immigrant honor killings, 118
Africa
    female genital mutilation, 139, 141–143, 147–152, 153
    gender imbalance, 137
    intimate partner violence, 46–50

Age
    elder abuse detection, 205–206
    intimate partner violence, 62
    parricide, 167–168, 172
Aggression and parricide, 174–175
agisra (organization), 156
Ahmad, Nehaluddin, 89–94
Alam, Shah, 99, 102
Alcohol. *See* Substance abuse
Allan, Alfred, 43
Allies Law Office, 66
Alon, Sara, 199
Alzheimer's Care Centre (ACC), 207
Alzheimer's Disease Foundation Malaysia (ADFM), 207
Ameer, Hamza, 86
American Islamic Congress, 121
American Islamic Forum for Democracy, 121
Amnesty International, 46–50, 154–156
Andresen, Greg, 41–42
Anger, 25
Antisocial children, 168–170
Antisocial personality disorder, 169
Anxiety, 25
Arab Women's Legal Network, 126
Ariyathilaka, Kaushalya Ruwanthika, 95–104
Armenia, 135
Asha, Enaam, 126

226

Index

Asia
    dowry-related violence, 80–88, 89–94, 95–104
    elder abuse, 187–192, 201–207, 210
    female genital mutilation, 142, 153
    girl babies are victims of family violence, 130–137
    intimate partner violence, 51–55, 64–70

Asian Americans
    elder abuse, 208–214
    gender imbalance, 136

Asian Pacific Islander Legal Outreach, 213

Aswad, Du'a Khalil, 107, 109

Aswad, Khalil, 107

Asylum and female genital mutilation, 157

Aurat Foundation, 112

Australia, 38–45

Azerbaijan, 135

B

Balkan immigrant honor killings, 118

Balkan states, 133, 136

Bangladesh, 95–104

Bangladesh immigrant honor killings, 118

Barakat, Ihssan, 124–126

The Battered Woman Syndrome, 114–115

Begum, Hafeeza, 99, 102

Begum, Shaheen, 99, 100, 102

Behavior problems and child abuse, 55

Beijing Declaration and Platform for Action, 85

Benin, 143

Betron, Myra, 49

Birth complications, 101, 139, 141, 151, 156

Bisexuals. *See* LGBT (Lesbian, gay, bisexual, and transgender people)

Bladder infections, 141

Blame, self
    elder abuse, 182–183
    intimate partner violence, 26, 28

Blaming the victim
    children, 34
    Ireland, 34
    Japan, 67–68
    Nigeria, 48
    Tanzania, 49

The Body Shop, 66

Boundary setting, 171–173, 175

Bride burning
    India, 89–94
    Pakistan, 84–85, 86
    See also Dowry-related violence

British Crime Survey (2000), 17

British Medical Journal, 133–134

Brown, Sandra, 57–58

Bryant, Gary, 44

Buddhists, 111–112

Burkina Faso, 143

Burning, brides. *See* Bride burning

Burning, self, 107–108

C

CAIR (Council on American-Islamic Relations), 114, 121

Cameroon, 143

Canada
    divorce-related violence, 159–163
    elder abuse, 192
    female genital mutilation, 142

227

honor killings, 113, 114, 115, 121
intimate partner violence, 17
Canadian Islamic Congress, 113
CARE (Chinese Americans Restoring Elders Project), 210
Carmona, Richard H., 15, 17
Carroll, Mustafaa, 114
CASS (Chinese Academy of Social Sciences), 132, 133
Caste system and dowry-related violence, 92, 94
Catastrophic events, 35–36
Caucasus, 133
CDC (Centers for Disease Control and Prevention), 15, 17
CEDAW (Convention on the Elimination of All Forms of Discrimination Against Women), 85–86
Celi, Elizabeth, 41–42, 44
Centers for Disease Control and Prevention (CDC), 15, 17
Central African Republic, 143
Chad, 143
Chebet, Ana, 150
Chebet, Kokop, 149
Chelangat, John, 148–149
Chemical abuse, 16, 26, 167, 205
Chemutai, Alice, 150–151
Cheng, Peter, 211, 212
Chesler, Phyllis, 110–121
Child abduction, 160–163
Child abuse
China, 130–137
cycle, 17, 18, 24, 34, 55
deaths, 115
divorce-related violence, 159–163
Ireland, 34
parricide, 165–169
therapy, 16
Turkey, 14
United Kingdom, 17
Vietnam, 55
See also Female genital mutilation; Honor killings
Child Act (2001) (Malaysia), 202
Child marriage, 101, 119
Childbirth complications, 101, 139, 141, 151, 156
Children
antisocial, 168–170
divorce-related violence, 159–163
intimate partner violence, 24, 28, 34, 42, 54, 74
mentally ill, 168, 169–170
parricide, 164–176
rights, 139–140, 144–145, 154
See also Child abuse; Female genital mutilation; Honor killings
China, 130–137
Chinese Academy of Social Sciences (CASS), 132, 133
Chinese Americans
elder abuse, 208–214
gender imbalance, 136
Chinese Americans Restoring Elders (CARE) Project, 210
Christians, 111–112
Chronic conditions
elder abuse risk factor, 203, 207
resulting from abuse, 16, 22–23
Circumcision, female. See Female genital mutilation
Civil society organizations (CSOs), 86–87
Classism, 73, 75
See also Socioeconomic class
Clitoridectomy, 140

See also Female genital mutilation
Clyde, Scotland, 57, 58
Communism
   gender imbalance, 133, 135–136
   intimate partner violence, 67
Community involvement in honor killings, 115–117
Concentration problems, 25
Conduct disorder, 169
Confusion and elder abuse, 182
Consumerism and dowry-related violence, 93
Convention on the Elimination of All Forms of Discrimination Against Women (CEDAW), 85–86
Côte d'Ivoire, 143
Council on American-Islamic Relations (CAIR), 114, 121
Counseling
   elder abuse, 184
   intimate partner violence, 54
   See also Therapy
Court protection and elder abuse, 185
Criminalization
   female genital mutilation, 148
   honor killings, 107, 123–127
   intimate partner violence, 65
   marital rape, 54
Cruelty to Women Ordinance (1983) (Bangladesh), 98
CSOs (civil society organizations), 86–87
Cultural pressures
   dowry, 83–84
   elder abuse, 211, 213
   female genital mutilation, 142–144, 149–150, 151–152
   intimate partner violence, 28, 68
Custody, child, 28, 36–37, 42, 159–163
Cycles of violence, 17, 18, 24, 34, 55

D

Dang Vung Nguyen, 54
Das Gupta, Monica, 137
Davies, Caroline, 108
de Caestecker, Linda, 58–59
Deaths
   child abuse, 115
   female genital mutilation, 101, 139, 141, 151
   See also Homicides
DELTA (Domestic Violence Prevention Enhancement and Leadership Through Alliances), 17
Delusions and parricide, 169–170
Demographic and Health Surveys, 143
Denial
   honor killings, 113–114
   intimate partner violence, 28
Depression
   elder abuse, 182
   intimate partner violence, 25
   parricide, 169
Deprivation, 74
   See also Neglect
Diallo, Aissatou, 155, 157–158
Discipline, child, 171–173
Divorce
   child-directed violence, 159–163
   dowry-related violence, 99, 100
   intimate partner violence, 26–27

Family Violence

"Domestic Abuse of Women and Men in Ireland" (report), 14
Domestic violence. *See* Child abuse; Elder abuse; Family violence; Intimate partner violence
Domestic Violence Act 1994 (Malaysia), 202
Domestic Violence Law (2001) (Japan), 65
Domestic Violence Prevention Enhancement and Leadership Through Alliances (DELTA), 17
Domination in intimate partner violence, 24–25, 73–75
Dong, Xinqi, 209, 210, 211
Dowry Prohibition Act (1980) (Bangladesh), 98
Dowry Prohibition Act (1961) (India), 90
Dowry-related violence
    Bangladesh, 95–104
    elder abuse, 191
    India, 89–94, 191
    Pakistan, 80–88

E

Ebenezer, Esther G., 201–207
Eberstadt, Nick, 133
Economic and Social Research Institute (ESRI) (Ireland), 14, 33
Economics
    development costs, 16–17, 101–102
    dowry-related violence, 83, 91, 97–98, 100–102
The Economist, 130–137
Edith Cowan University, 40–41, 43
Education
    dowry-related violence, 92, 101
    girls' mortality rates, 137

honor killings, 120–121, 125
intimate partner violence, 75
Edwards, Alan, 39, 42, 43, 44–45
Egypt, 143
Egyptian immigrant honor killings, 118
Elder abuse
    Canada, 192
    Chinese Americans, 208–214
    elders must seek help, 179–186
    Europe, 192
    films, 196–197
    India, 187–192
    Israel, 193–200
    Malaysia, 201–207
    overview, 180–183
    reactions, 182–184
    risk factors, 203, 205, 207
    signs, 184, 200, 205–206
    types, 180–182, 199, 203–204
    United Kingdom, 188, 192
    United States, 15, 188, 192, 208–214
"Elder Abuse" (article), 15
Elder Abuse Awareness Day, 188
Elmasry, Mohamed, 113
Embarrassment
    elder abuse, 183
    intimate partner violence, 26, 28
    See also Shame
Emotional abuse
    elders, 181, 189, 210
    intimate partner violence, 27, 41–42, 66, 74
Employment and intimate partner violence, 74, 75
End FGM campaign, 154–155, 156
Eritrea, 143
ESRI (Economic and Social Research Institute) (Ireland), 14, 33
Ethiopia, 143

Europe, 153–158
  elder abuse, 192
  female genital mutilation, 142, 153–158
  honor killings, 112, 115, 117–120
European Commission, 157
Excision in female genital mutilation, 140
Exploitation, financial. *See* Financial abuse, control and manipulation
Eze-Anaba, Itoro, 48

F

Face saving and elder abuse, 212–213
FAD (Fight Against Dowry), 87
Failure and male victims, 41–42
Familial piety, 211, 212
Family Law Reporting Pilot Project, 36
Family therapy, 176
Family violence
  defined, 14, 23
  economic costs, 16–17, 101–102
  history, 23–24
  overview, 21–30
  See also Child abuse; Dowry-related violence; Elder abuse; Female genital mutilation; Honor killings; Intimate partner violence; Parricide
"Family Violence as a Public Health Issue" (speech), 15
Fatwas, 97
Fear
  dowry-related violence, 98, 99
  elder abuse, 182–184, 199, 209
  intimate partner violence, 25, 28, 42, 66, 75

Feldner, Yotam, 112–113
Female circumcision. *See* Female genital mutilation
Female genital mutilation
  Africa, 139, 141–143, 147–152, 153
  Asia, 142, 153
  Europe, 142, 153–158
  North America, 142
  WHO's call for elimination, 138–146
Fidelity and female genital mutilation, 142
Fight Against Dowry (FAD), 87
Filial piety, 211, 212
Filipino-American gender imbalance, 136
Films about elder abuse, 196–197
Financial abuse, control and manipulation
  elders, 181, 189, 191, 195, 199, 203–204, 208, 210
  intimate partner violence, 25, 28, 40, 69, 74
Finlay, Fergus, 34
Firearms, 167, 174
Forbes, Geraldine, 93
Forced marriage, 119
France
  female genital mutilation, 155
  honor killings, 119
Fraud schemes, 204
Friends and family
  honor killings, 115–117
  intimate partner violence, 28
Frustration tolerance, 173
Fukushima, Mizuho, 66–67

G

Gays. *See* LGBT (Lesbian, gay, bisexual, and transgender people)

GDP (Gross domestic product), 16–17
Gender-based violence. *See* Dowry-related violence; Female genital mutilation; Gender imbalances; Honor killings; Intimate partner violence
Gender discrimination as factor in violence
    Bangladesh, 97–98
    dowry-related violence, 81–83, 93, 97–98
    elder abuse, 189–190
    female genital mutilation, 157
    gender imbalance, 130–137
    honor killings, 106–109
    India, 93
    intimate partner violence, 49, 68
    Iraq, 106–109
    Japan, 68
    Nigeria, 49
    Pakistan, 81–83
    Tanzania, 49
Gender identity, 75
Gender imbalances, 130–137, 135*t*
Gendercide. *See* Gender imbalances
General Statistics Office of Vietnam, 51–55
Genital mutilation. *See* Female genital mutilation
Georgia, 135
Germany
    female genital mutilation, 155, 156
    honor killings, 119
Ghana, 143
Gifts, 27
Girls, abortions of, 130–137
Glasgow, Scotland, 57, 58
Grimaldi and Yeung, 211

Gross domestic product, 16–17
Guedalia, Judith, 194
Guilt, 182–183
    See also Self-blame
Guinea, 143
Guns, 167, 174

H

Habitual residence, 160, 162
Hague Convention, 161, 163
Halperin, Sarah, 195–199
Hamilton, Graeme, 159–163
Hang, Tran Thi, 52
Harassment, 75, 97
Haryana, India, 136
HCRP (Human Rights Commission of Pakistan), 84
Health care
    costs, 15–16
    withholding in elder abuse, 189, 190, 200, 204–205, 206
Health care professionals
    elder abuse, 185, 200, 202, 203, 205–207
    female genital mutilation, 139, 144, 146, 151, 156
    intimate partner violence, 43, 54, 57–61
    parricide, 170–171, 175–176
Health effects
    female genital mutilation, 139, 140–141, 148, 155–156
    intimate partner violence, 22–23, 53–55
Health Service Executive (HSE) (Ireland), 32, 35–36
Heide, Kathleen M., 164–176
Helplessness, 26
Heterosexism, 77
Hindus, 112, 118

HIV/AIDS
　　female genital mutilation, 151
　　intimate partner violence, 73
H'Mong, 53
Homicides
　　Bangladesh, 95–104
　　Canada, 113
　　children, 115, 159–163
　　dowry-related, 84–88, 89–94, 95–104
　　female infants, 131
　　honor killings, 105–109, 110–121, 122–127
　　India, 89–94
　　Iraq, 105–109
　　Ireland, 35, 37
　　Jordan, 112, 113, 122–127
　　Lebanon, 124
　　Nigeria, 47–48
　　Pakistan, 84–85, 112
　　parricide, 164–176
　　Scotland, 63
　　United States, 110–121, 159–163, 164–176
Homophobia, 73, 75, 77
Homosexuals. *See* LGBT (Lesbian, gay, bisexual, and transgender people)
Honor killings
　　Canada, 113, 114, 115, 121
　　defined, 114
　　Europe, 112, 115, 117–120
　　Iraq, 105–109
　　Jordan, 112, 113, 122–127
　　Lebanon, 124
　　Pakistan, 112
　　United States, 110–121
Hopelessness, 26
Hormones, stress, 174–175
Hotlines
　　elder abuse, 184, 185
　　male victims of intimate partner violence, 43
Housing
　　elder abuse, 185, 195
　　intimate partner violence, 28, 74
HSE (Health Service Executive) (Ireland), 32, 35–36
Hudood ordinance, 87
Human Rights Commission of Pakistan (HCRP), 84
Human Rights Watch, 124
Human trafficking, 97
Hunt, Carol, 31–37
Hussein, Begard, 109
Hussein, Hassan, 108
Hussein, Haydar, 108
Hussein, Leila, 108
Husseini, Rana, 122–123, 124, 127
Hypervigilance, 26

I

ICPD (International Conference on Population and Development), 85
Illahi, Naheeda Mahboob, 85
Immigrants
　　elder abuse, 208–214
　　female genital mutilation, 142, 155–158
　　honor killings, 114–115, 118–121
　　intimate partner violence, 73, 75
India, 89–94, 187–192
　　abuse of older people by family members is increasing, 187–192
　　bride burning is a significant problem, 89–94
　　gender imbalance, 133, 136–137

Family Violence

Indochina Sino-American Community Center, 211, 213–214
Infanticide, 131
Infertility
    female genital mutilation, 141
    gender imbalance, 133
Infibulation, 140
    See also Female genital mutilation
Information and Research Center of the King Hussein Foundation, 125
International Conference on Population and Development (ICPD), 85
Intimate Partner Abuse of Men, 40–41
Intimate partner violence
    Australia, 38–45
    Canada, 17
    defined, 23, 73
    differs from honor killings, 114–117
    effect on children, 14, 24, 34, 36, 54
    health care professionals, 43, 54, 57–61
    history, 23–24
    Ireland, 14, 31–37
    Japan, 64–70
    LGBT, 23, 71–77
    male victims, 33, 35, 38–45, 71–77
    Nigeria, 46–50
    overview, 21–30
    reasons victims stay, 28–29
    Scotland, 56–63
    tactics, 24–25, 40–41, 73, 74–76
    Tanzania, 49
    United Kingdom, 17, 56–63
    United States, 21–30, 71–77, 114
    Vietnam, 51–55
    See also Dowry-related violence
Iraq, 105–109
Iraqi immigrant honor killings, 118
Ireland, 31–37
    intimate partner violence, 14
    women bear the brunt of family violence, 31–37
IRIN (Integrated Regional Information Networks), 46–50
Islam
    dowry-related violence, 82, 87, 97
    honor killings, 106, 107–109, 110–121
Islamic Society of North America, 121
Isolation
    elder abuse, 184, 191, 195, 207
    intimate partner violence, 24–25, 40–41, 74, 76
Israel, 193–200
Ivory Coast, 143

J

Jahez. *See* Dowry-related violence
Jansen, Henrica A.F.M., 53
Japan, 64–70
    elder abuse, 210
    spousal abuse remains hidden, 64–70
Japanese Americans, gender imbalance, 136
"Jekyll and Hyde" personality, 27
Jews, 111–112
Jordan, 122–127
    cracks down on honor killings, 122–127
    leniency for honor killings, 112, 113

Journal of the American Geriatrics Society, 198
Judd, Terri, 105–109

K

Karim, Fauzia, 103
Kenya, 143
Khalife, Nadya, 124
Khan, Saira Rahman, 97–98, 103–104
Khushhali Bank, 86
Kikwete, Jakaya, 49
Killings. *See* Homicides; Honor Killings
King Abdullah II of Jordan, 124
King Hussein Foundation, 125
Kinh, 53
Knives, 174–175
Kokop, Alice, 149, 151
Korean-Asians, 135
"Kosians," 135
Krantz, Gunilla, 54
Kurdish immigrant honor killings, 118

L

Laberge, Marie-Christine, 161
Labia majora, 140
    See also Female genital mutilation
Labia minora, 140
    See also Female genital mutilation
Lagos, Nigeria, 46–50
Latif, Aamir, 112
Latin America, 153
The Law of Marriage Act (1971) (Tanzania), 49
Leaving, dangers, 27, 34–36
Lebanon, 124
Lebel, Helene, 160–161, 163
LEDAP (Legal Defence and Assistance Project), 48
Lee, Gin, 210, 213–214
Legal administrative abuse, 41
Legal bias, perceptions, 36–37
Legal Defence and Assistance Project (LEDAP), 48
Lesbians. *See* LGBT (Lesbian, gay, bisexual, and transgender people)
LGBT (Lesbian, gay, bisexual, and transgender people), 23, 71–77
Liu, Jinfu, 209–210
Loudes, Christine, 154–155, 157

M

Macedonia, 136
Mahmoud, Houzan, 107, 109
Maintenance and Welfare of Parents and Senior Citizens Act (2007) (India), 192
Malaysia, 201–207
Male domination and superiority. *See* Gender discrimination as factor in violence
Mali, 143
Marital rape, 50, 54
Marriage
    child, 101, 119
    female genital mutilation, 142
    forced, 119
    See also Dowry-related violence
Mary (Scottish abuse victim), 61–62
Massachusetts, 114
Matricide, 172, 173–174
    See also Parricide
"Matricide: A Critique of the Literature" (article, Heide), 168
Matsumoto, Chie, 64–70

Mauritania, 143
Mayes, Andrea, 38–45
McNeill, David, 64–70
McSweeney, Robyn, 43
Media
    dowry-related violence, 87, 88
    honor killings, 126
    intimate partner violence, 44, 54
Men, violence victims
    Australia, 38–45
    gay, bisexual, and transgender, 71–77
    Ireland, 33, 35
    United States, 71–77
    See also Elder abuse
Menna, Amy, 76
Men's Advisory Network, 44
Mental health costs, 16
Mental illness
    parricide, 168–170
    risk factor, 16
Microcredit, 86
MICS (Multiple Indicator Cluster Survey), 143
Middle East
    elder abuse, 193–200
    female genital mutilation, 142, 143, 153
    gender imbalance, 137
    honor killings, 105–109, 112, 113, 122–127
Mikala, Stephane, 47
Ministry of Integration (Netherlands), 120
Mood swings, 27
Mortality. See Deaths
Multiple Indicator Cluster Survey (MICS), 143
Murder. See Homicides
Murder in the Name of Honor, 123
Musaji, Sheila, 113

Museveni, Yoweri, 148
Muslim-American associations, 121
Muslim-Canadian associations, 121
Muslims. See Islam
Mustafa, Mohammed, 109
Mutilation, genital. See Female genital mutilation

N

Nair, Ajay, 113–114
Nakano, Mami, 67
Namazie, Matyam, 119–120
National Center for Victims of Crime (United States), 21–30
National Coalition of Anti-Violence Programs (United States), 71–77
National Commission for Women (India), 90
National Crime Council (Ireland), 14, 33
National Crime Record Bureau of India (NCRB), 90
National Health Service (Scotland), 57
National Institute of Justice (United States), 15
National Plan of Action (Pakistan), 86
National Study on Domestic Violence Against Women in Vietnam, 51–55
National Violence Against Women Survey (United States), 76
NCRB (National Crime Record Bureau of India), 90
Nefesh Israel, 194, 197–199
Neglect
    child, 14, 165

defined, 182
elder, 15, 182, 189–190, 200, 203–205, 210
See also Child abuse; Elder abuse
Netherlands honor killings, 120, 121
Newman, Matthew, 157
Nguyen, Dang Vung, 54
Niger, 143
Nigeria, 46–50
family violence affects many women, 46–50
female genital mutilation, 143
"Nigeria: Unheard Voices" (report), 47–50
Nightmares, 25
Nimat, Sara Jaffar, 108
Nomaki, Masako, 67
Normal, violence accepted as
elder neglect, 190
intimate partner violence, 28, 49, 53, 76
See also Cultural pressures
North America. *See* Canada; United States
Numbness, 26

O

Obasanjo, Olusegun, 50
Odhikar, 98
Olive, Jean Marc, 53
One-child policy, 136
See also Gender imbalances
One in Three campaign, 41
"One Law for All. A Campaign Against Shari'a Law in Britain," 119–120
Oppositional defiant disorder, 169
O'Reilly, Joe, 37
Osman, Narmin, 107

Ostergren, Per-Olof, 54
Outing, 75

P

Pakistan, 80–88
child marriage, 119
dowry disputes lead to violence, 80–88
gender imbalance, 137
honor killings, 112
Pakistan immigrant honor killings, 118
Palestinian immigrant honor killings, 118
Parental respect, 171–173
Parricide, 164–176
Parveen, Rakhshinda, 80–88
Parvez, Aqsa, 113
Perisic, Danyela, 160–163
Perisic, Deyan, 160–163
Perisic, Nenad, 162
Perisic, Predag, 160–163
Perpetrators
elder abuse, 180, 205
intimate partner violence, 26–27, 36–37, 55
Peter, Tom, 122–127
Pets, 74
Piety, familial, 211, 212
See also Elder abuse
Police
dowry-related violence, 99
intimate partner violence, 17, 43, 48, 65, 67, 77
Post-traumatic stress disorder (PTSD), 16, 25, 169
Poverty
dowry-related violence, 103–104
honor killings, 125

Pregnant women, 55
  See also Birth complications
Prema (elder abuse victim), 188
Property and elder abuse, 195
Psychological abuse
  elders, 181, 189, 203–204
  intimate partner violence, 27, 66
  matricide, 173
Psychosis and parricide, 169–170
PTSD (post-traumatic stress disorder), 16, 25, 169
Punjab, India gender imbalance, 136, 137

Q

Queen Rania of Jordan, 124
Queer identity, 75–76
Quinn, Mary, 161

R

Race, 73, 75
Rania, Queen, 124
Rape
  Bangladesh, 97
  honor killings, 116
  Iraq, 106, 109
  Japan, 50, 54
  LGBT, 75, 76
  marital, 50, 54
  Nigeria, 47, 48
  Tanzania, 49
  United States, 75, 76
  See also Sexual abuse
Rauf, Shawbo Ali, 106
Reding, Viviane, 157
Religion
  dowry-related violence, 82, 87, 97
  female genital mutilation, 142–144, 154
  honor killings, 106–109, 110–121
  intimate partner violence, 28, 75
Reporting, reluctance
  all types, 15
  dowry-related violence, 84
  elder abuse, 182–184, 189, 195, 198, 201–207, 212–213
  intimate partner violence, 40, 42, 53, 66
  rape, 109
Residence, habitual, 160, 162
Respite programs, 185, 207
Restraining orders, 69
Rights
  children's, 139–140, 144–145, 154
  elders, 192, 199
  See also Women's rights
Risk factors
  elder abuse, 189, 198–199, 203, 205, 207
  family violence, 16
  intimate partner violence, 55
  parricide, 167
  See also Cycles of violence
Rosen, Leah, 194
Rozario, Santi, 100

S

Sabiny tribe (Uganda), 147–152
SACHET (Society for the Advancement of Community, Health, Education, and Training), 80, 84, 87
Safety
  elder abuse, 183–185, 206–207
  intimate partner violence, 27, 35–36
San Francisco, CA, 211, 213
Sandal, Kandeela, 113

Index

Sarhan, Afif, 108
Schweiger, Laura, 153–158
Scotland, 56–63
Self-blame
   elder abuse, 182–183
   intimate partner violence, 26, 28
Self-esteem
   perpetrators, 26–27, 69
   victims, 25, 28
Self-Help for the Elderly, 211–212, 213
Self-identity
   LGBT, 75
   perpetrators, 26–27
   victims, 25, 41–42, 75
Self-immolation, 107–108
Senior citizen abuse. *See* Elder abuse
Sentencing
   female genital mutilation, 151
   honor killings in Jordan, 123–127
Serbia, 136
Setting boundaries, 171–173, 175
Sex-determination technology, 133
   See also Gender imbalances
Sex ratio discrepancy. *See* Gender imbalances
Sexual abuse
   children, 16
   dowry-related, 97
   elders, 181, 195, 199, 203–204
   intimate partner violence, 40, 75
   LGBT, 75
   See also Rape
Sexual discrepancy. *See* Gender imbalances
Sexual Offences Special Provisions Act (1998) (Tanzania), 49
Sexual orientation, 75
   See also LGBT (Lesbian, gay, bisexual, and transgender people)
Sexually transmitted diseases, 75
Shaheen (Bangladesh victim), 95–96
Shame
   dowry-related violence, 85
   elder abuse, 182–183, 199, 206, 209
   intimate partner violence, 26, 28, 39, 41–42, 53, 66
   male victims, 39, 41–42
Shankardass, Mala Kapur, 187–192
Sharia law
   honor killings, 108–109
   UK movement against, 119–120
   See also Islam
Sharif, Nawaz, 87
Sharma, Shri, 83
Shelters, 24, 77, 120–121
Shibusawa, Tazuko, 210
Shohag, Mohhamed, 95–96, 99
Shulak, Jonathan, 163
Shunning, 111–112
Siegel-Itzkovich, Judy, 193–200
Sikhs, 112, 118
Silence
   dowry-related violence, 85, 99
   elder abuse, 182–183, 209–210, 212–213
   family violence, 15
   intimate partner violence, 53, 56–63, 64–70, 77
   LGBT, 77
   See also Reporting, reluctance
Singapore, 133
Single-parent families and matricide, 173–174
Sisterhood Is Global Institute, 126
Sium, Shewa, 156

Sleep problems, 25
Social pressure. *See* Cultural pressures
Social withdrawal, 26
    See also Isolation
Society for the Advancement of Community, Health, Education, and Training (SACHET), 80, 84, 87
Socioeconomic class
    dowry-related violence, 83, 91, 93–94, 103–104
    honor killings, 125
    intimate partner violence, 22, 57–63, 73, 75
Son preference. *See* Gender imbalances
SoundVision.com, 113
South Africa, 192
South America, 153
South Korea, 133, 134–135
Spousal abuse. *See* Intimate partner violence
Srinivas, M.N., 92–93
Stabbings, 174–175
Stalking, 75, 76
State of the World Population Fact Sheet (2005), 17
Staying, reasons, 28–29, 34
Stealing, 74
Stigma
    female genital mutilation, 158
    honor killings, 113, 117
    intimate partner violence, 53, 57–58, 77
    LGBT, 77
Stove burnings. *See* Bride burning
Stress hormones and parricide, 174–175
Stroke Centre (Malaysia), 207
Subotic, Zivorad, 162–163
Substance abuse, 16, 26, 167, 205

Sudan, 143
Suicide
    children, 168
    dowry-related, 90, 94
    intimate partner violence, 42, 55, 75
Sun, Yuying, 213–214
Support for elder abuse, 184–186
Support groups
    elder abuse, 184, 195, 207
    intimate partner violence, 54
Suzuki, Fumi, 66, 68–69
Sweden, 119

T

Tagg, Mairead, 59–61
Taiwan, 133, 134
Takahashi, Tokie, 68
Takeshita, Akiko, 212–213
Tanzania
    female genital mutilation, 143
    intimate partner violence, 49
Taxes, 17
Therapy, 16, 176
    See also Counseling
Thompson, Tanya, 56–63
Threats, 28
Tibet, 133
Tolerance, frustration, 173
Toolis, Kevin, 162
Tran Thi Hang, 54
Transgender people. *See* LGBT (Lesbian, gay, bisexual, and transgender people)
Transphobia, 73, 77
Turkey, 14
Turkish immigrant honor killings, 118

Index

U

Uganda, 147–152
UNICEF, 144–145
United Kingdom
    child abuse, 17
    divorce-related violence, 162
    elder abuse, 188, 192
    female genital mutilation, 155
    honor killings, 119–120, 121
    intimate partner violence, 17, 56–63
United Nations
    Convention on the Elimination of All Forms of Discrimination Against Women, 85–86
    economic costs of violence, 17
    female genital mutilation statement, 144–145
    honor killing statistics, 112
    National Study on Domestic Violence Against Women in Vietnam, 51–55
United Nations Children's Health Fund (UNICEF), 144–145
United Nations Population Fund (UNFPA), 17, 112, 144–145
United States, 21–30, 71–77, 110–121, 164–176, 208–214
    Chinese senior citizens suffer from elder abuse, 208–214
    divorce-related violence, 159–163
    elder abuse, 15, 188, 192, 208–214
    female genital mutilation, 142
    gender imbalance, 136
    honor killings should be differentiated from domestic violence, 110–121
    intimate partner violence, 21–30, 71–77, 114
    lesbian, gay, bisexual, and transgender (LGBT) people experience abuse, 23, 71–77
    overview of family violence, 21–30
    parricide, 164–176
UNPFA (United Nations Population Fund), 17, 112, 144–145
Urinary tract infections, 141

V

Verbal abuse
    elders, 189, 199
    intimate partner violence, 66, 74
Victim assistance programs, elder abuse, 184–185
Vietnam, 51–55
Violence, family. *See* Family violence
Violence against women. *See* Dowry-related violence; Female genital mutilation; Honor killings; Intimate partner violence
Virginity and female genital mutilation, 142
Virility and honor killings, 113
Vucerakovich, Vera, 161

W

Walker, Lenore, 114–115
Warren, Mary Anne, 132
Weddings. *See* Dowry-related violence
Weill Cornell Medical College, 179–186
WHO. *See* World Health Organization (WHO)
Why Kids Kill Parents: Child Abuse and Adolescent Homicide, 165
Widow abuse, 190–191
    See also Elder abuse

Wife abuse. *See* Intimate partner violence
Wikan, Unni, 114
Womakuyu, Frederick, 147–152
Women, violence against. *See* Dowry-related violence; Female genital mutilation; Honor killings; Intimate partner violence
Women and Children Repression Prevention Act (2000) (Bangladesh), 98
Women's Aid (Ireland), 35
Women's rights
    Bangladesh, 97–98
    dowry-related violence, 86, 97–98
    female genital mutilation, 139–140, 144–145, 148, 154
    honor killings, 107–108, 119
    intimate partner violence, 23–24, 54
    Iraq, 107–108
    Pakistan, 86
Wong, Vivien, 212, 213
World Elder Abuse Awareness Day, 188
World Health Assembly, 145–146
World Health Organization (WHO)
    calls for the elimination of female genital mutilation, 138–146
    family violence prevention, 15, 17–18
World Medical Association, 14

X

Xiaoqing, Rong, 208–214
Xue, Xinran, 131

Y

Yazidi tribe, 107
Yemen, 137
Yeung-Ha, Pauline, 211
Yoshida, Emi, 65, 69–70

Z

Zia-ul-Haq, Muhammad, 87

www.ingramcontent.com/pod-product-compliance
Lightning Source LLC
Chambersburg PA
CBHW071905290426
44110CB00013B/1287